In humility we offer
this to
Swami Sivananda Saraswati,
who
inspired and guided
Swami Satyananda Saraswati
through his
Tirth Yatra.

यह जीवन एक चित्र है,
किसी तूलिका का जीवन्त चमत्कार।

जीवन के कलाकार,
अपनी तूलिका से नव-जीवन के चित्र बनाओ,
इन चित्रों के स्त्री-पुरुष-बालकों में,
हँसी, खुशी, मुस्कान,
मस्ती खिला दो।

चित्र के दीपक,
हमारी तीर्थ-यात्रा में झलक जाओ,
अपने सूक्ष्म मानस में अन्धा यात्री,
तिमिर रात्री के तीर्थाटन में
चिर-उज्ज्वल
और चिर-अमर बना दो।

मार्ग बन्धु,
तुम्हारे चित्रों की गंगोत्री का मार्ग अनन्त है,
इसकी उपत्यकाएँ अगम्य।
इसके पन्थी कोई-कोई।
हम कब पहुचेंगे।
बतलाओगे ?

हमने थोड़ा सा मार्ग पार कर लिया है,
कुछ उतार चढ़ाव पार कर लिए हैं,
कुछ घाटियाँ पार कर ली हैं,
पर अभी भी यात्रा शेष है,

तुम अपने चित्रों से प्रेरणा दो,
और
अपने चरणों की छाया में,
हमें तीर्थ करा दो।

Life is a canvas of myriad colours,
A living, breathing miracle of the creator.

O Artist of life!
With your masterstroke
Paint new life
And let your images radiate laughter,
Happiness and joy

O Light who lends radiance to my portrait!
Manifest yourself in this tirth yatra of mine,
Throw perpetual light and bestow your grace
On this ignorant traveller
Who is a pilgrim seeking light and knowledge
On a dark and treacherous path.

O Companion on this path!
Unending is the journey of
Your vast creation;
Few are the travellers who can reach
The inaccessible terrains;
Tell me will I ever reach the destination!

I have covered some of the harrowing path,
Overcoming the obstacles that befell me
And also crossed the low-lying abyss,
But my journey is still incomplete.

Inspire me with your beautiful creations
And lead me in the
Shadow of your footsteps
Through this pilgrimage of mine.

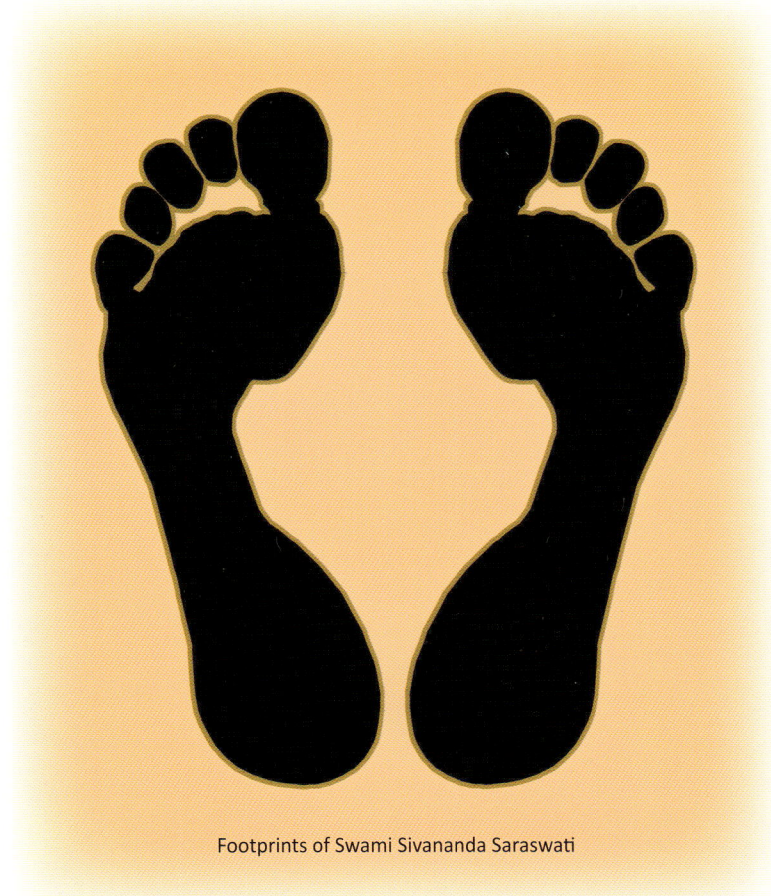

Footprints of Swami Sivananda Saraswati

Tirth Yatra 1

Swami Satyanand

फूल फूल से बनती माला,
सुन्दर, सुरभित, कोमल, पावन।
भावों के सुन्दर फूलों को चुन कर
यह माला अर्पण है – भक्तों को।।

CONTENTS

The terms Satyananda Yoga® and Bihar Yoga® are registered trademarks owned by International Yoga Fellowship Movement (IYFM). The use of the same in this book is with permission and should not in any way be taken as affecting the validity of the marks.

Published by Yoga Publications Trust
   First edition 2007
   Reprinted 2013

ISBN: 978-81-86336-62-5

Publisher and distributor: Yoga Publications Trust, Ganga Darshan, Munger, Bihar.
Website: www.biharyoga.net

Printed by Kraftwerk, Gurgaon, at Aegean Offset Printers, Greater Noida.

Once whilst in flight, gliding majestically
over the deepest recesses of endless space,
the rare Homa bird laid its eggs.
Even as the eggs fell into the fathomless akasha,
chicks emerged and, fluttering their tiny little wings,
flew into the void, crying out for their mother.

There was one, however, who took a different path.
This lone harbinger came down to the mortal realms
to spread the message of immortality and light;
He was called Satyam – Swami Satyananda Saraswati.

गंभीर गगनगामी होमा पक्षी ने तीन-चार अण्डे
जने—शून्य आकाश में ही। वे गिरने लगे। रास्ते में ही
इनसे पंख-युक्त बच्चे फूट निकले।

कुछ तो चल पड़े आकाश की ओर—माँ, माँ की रट
लगाते और एक चल पड़ा मृत्युलोक की ओर,
अमरत्व का सन्देश सुनाने और वही है—
सत्यम्—स्वामी सत्यानन्द सरस्वती।

1923...

ALMORA: Janmabhoomi

Amidst the heavenly sky-kissing mountains of Almora,
where the nights are silvery and the days golden,
where a mysterious ambience envelopes the dawn,
where the golden rays of the sun create a dream,
there, enfolded in the lap of Mount Kailash,
a newborn child half opened his eyes and
from his lips resounded the sacred words:
Satyam, Shivam, Sundaram.

It seemed as if nature was present to bestow all her gifts on him;
Saraswati gave the child eloquence,
the cuckoo gave him sweetness,
the moon bestowed upon him its lustre,
and Usha, the harbinger of dawn, her decorative beauty.
Soon he grew into a gifted young student,
accomplished in literature, art and music.

Innate wisdom made him realize
that day is always followed by the darkness of night,
that streaks of lightning illumine the heavenly skies,
only to be swallowed by black clouds.
That the effulgence of the full moon
soon gives way to a dark foreboding moonless night.
That in the footsteps of a lush and verdant spring
follows the barrenness of winter.
That out of the cry of freedom arises the anguish of destruction.
That down the line of human history
rivers of blood have flowed in brutal massacres,
leaving humanity naked, vulnerable and exposed.

This vision of the impermanence of life gave way to viveka and vairagya.
He left in search of Shivam and reached Sivanandashram, Rishikesh.

For a young lad renunciation of wealth is difficult, women even more,
and name and fame most difficult of all.
Vultures fly high in the firmament,
seeking dead bodies on the ground,
but this bird of the infinite expanse of blue skies
was the worshipper of freedom.

He took the unshakeable vow
to walk the razor's edge of renunciation and surrender.
At an auspicious moment his inner self
called out to Guru for sannyasa.
The search for Shivam and Sundaram
brought him to his own self – Satyam,
Swami Satyananda Saraswati.

(Swami Jyotirmayananda, 1954)

अल्मोड़ा के स्वर्गिक प्रांगण में, जहाँ रातें चाँदी-सी और दिन सोने के होते हैं, जहाँ कुहेलिकामयी उषा रहस्यमयी प्रहेलिका का निर्माण करती, जहाँ सूर्य अपनी स्वर्णिम आभा से स्वप्निल समीरों का सृजन करता, वहीं कैलाश की गोद में इस शिशु नभचर ने अपनी अर्द्धोन्मीलित आँखें खोलीं और सहसा उसके मुख से निकल पड़ा—'सत्यं शिवं-सुन्दरम्।' सरस्वती ने उसे वरदान दिए। कोकिला ने अपनी मधुरता दी, चन्द्रमा ने अपनी ज्योत्सना और ऊषा ने दिए—अपने आभूषणों के उपहार। वह अल्पकाल में ही प्रतिभा सम्पन्न विद्यार्थी हो गया। साहित्य-संगीत-कला-विशारद।

दामिनी दमकी, स्वर्गिक सौन्दर्य का प्रवाह फूट पड़ा, परन्तु घन-घटा के घनघोर घोष में वह विलुप्त हो गयी। चाँद हँस पड़ा, परन्तु उसकी उसासों से अमावस्या की रात्रि सिक्त हो चुकी। वसंत की वासंतिकता शरद की निष्ठुरता में परिणत हो गयी। कुमुदिनी ने जल समाधि ग्रहण की। मोहक सौन्दर्य की विडम्बना ने शाश्वत सौन्दर्य की अलख जगायी।

नरमेघ का प्रारम्भ हुआ। रक्त की गंगा बही। मानवता ने दानवता के साथ नग्न प्रदर्शन किए। माली ने अर्द्धोन्मीलित पुष्पों को सहसा तोड़ दिया। जनजीवन की दयनीय दशा देख विवेक और वैराग्य ने मोह का मूलोच्छेदन किया। वह 'शिवं' की खोज में चल पड़ा और पहुँचा शिवानन्द आश्रम, ऋषिकेश।

कंचन का संन्यास कठिन है, कामिनी का संन्यास कठिनतर है और कठिनतम है यश और नाम का संन्यास। गिद्ध और चील भी आकाश में उड़ते हैं, परन्तु उनकी दृष्टि भी मृत-पिण्डों की ओर ही गड़ी रहती है। परन्तु यह पक्षी तो गंभीर गगन की स्वच्छन्दता का उपासक था, 'क्षुरस्य धारा निशिता दुरत्यया' के गहन पथ पर सतत् साहस के साथ चलते रहने की इसने भीष्म प्रतिज्ञा की और एक शुभ घड़ी में '...संन्यस्तं मया' की गंभीर गुरु गर्जना की। सुन्दरम् और शिवम् की खोज में चलने वाला युवक अब स्वयं 'सत्यम्' हो गया और उसका नाम पड़ा—
स्वामी सत्यानन्द सरस्वती।

(स्वामी ज्योतिर्मयानंद, 1954)

Swami Satyananda renounced his home and family in search of a guru. Soon after, he reached Rishikesh and there he met his spiritual master, Swami Sivananda Saraswati. During the twelve years that he spent with his guru, Swami Satyananda plunged himself into karma yoga and worked from dawn until late at night involving himself in every kind of work, from cleaning toilets to management of the ashram. Service to guru was his passion and joy.

Although he had a very keen intellect and his guru described him as a versatile genius, Swami Satyananda's learning did not come from formal instruction or study in the ashram. He followed with faith his guru's one command:

Work hard and you will be purified. You do not have to search for the light, the light will unfold from within you.

ॐ

26th July 1954

Few would have such Vairagya
at such a young age. Swami
Satyananda ji is full of the
Nachiketas - element. Yet,
any work that he takes up
he will complete in a perfect
manner. He does the work of
four people and yet never complains.
He is a versatile genius and a
linguist too. Yet, he is humble
and simple – an ideal Sadak
and Nishkamya Sevak. He
is a pillar of the Divine Life
Mission.

May God bless him with
health, long life, peace,
prosperity and Eternal Bliss.

Swami Sivananda

That is what happened. He gained an enlightened understanding of the secrets of spiritual life and became a foremost authority on yoga, tantra, Vedanta, Samkhya and kundalini. Seeing Swami Satyananda's natural ability to grasp, understand and explain profound esoteric and spiritual experiences with total clarity and simplicity, Swami Sivananda honoured his disciple by saying:

THE YOGA-VEDANTA FOREST UNIVERSITY

ANANDA KUTIR, RISHIKESH, HIMALAYAS, INDIA

ENQUIRE " WHO AM I "   I KNOW THE SELF ! !   AND BE FREE ! ! !

TAT TWAM ASI

WHEREAS, by the Grace of God, the Fountain of Eternal Bliss, and by the Will of the Almighty, it has been recognised that Sri SWAMI SATYANANDA is worthy of being awarded the sacred title of JNANA-YAJNOPABHRIT in appreciation of Meritorious services rendered in the field of **Dissemination of Spiritual Knowledge** and a firm devotion to Truth, Love and Purity, I hereby make this award in token of such recognition, with my best wishes and devout prayers to the Lord to bless the recipient hereof with health, long life, peace, prosperity, Eternal Bliss, success in all undertakings, Vidya, Tushti, Pushti and Divine Aiswarya.

This 7th day of September 1954.

Swami Sivananda

Chancellor

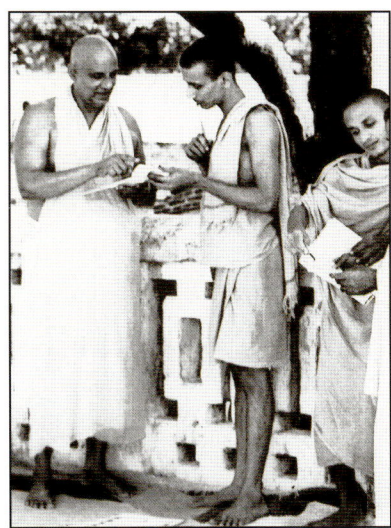

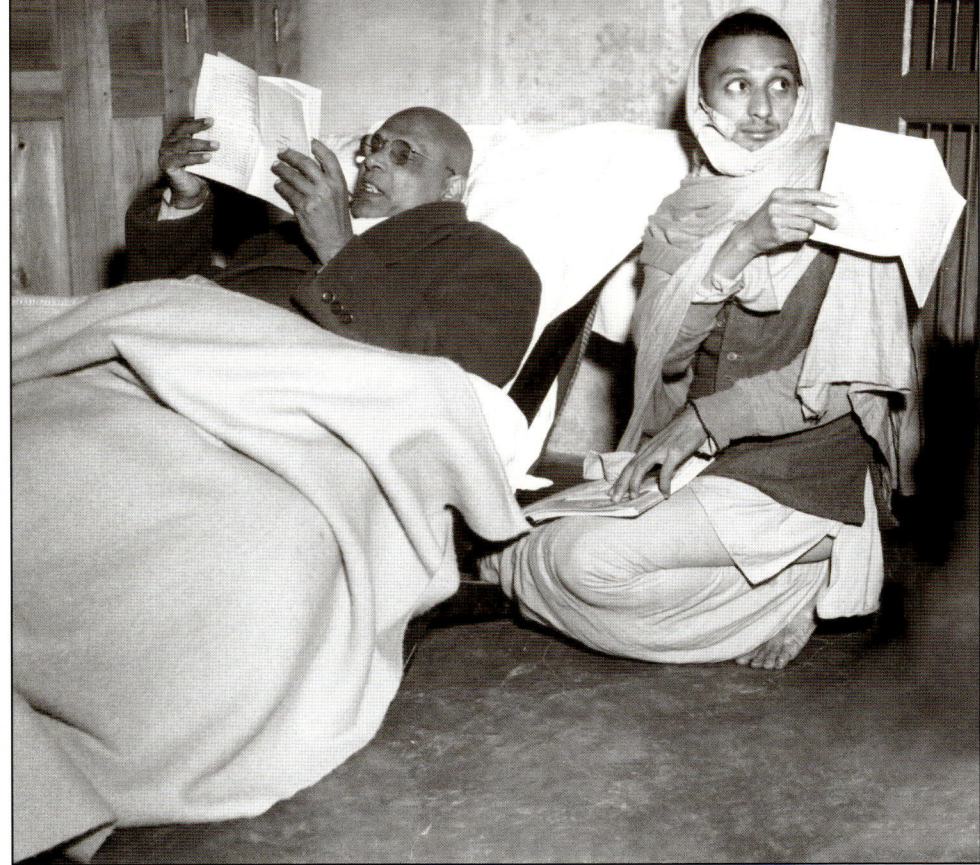

With guests and gurubhais

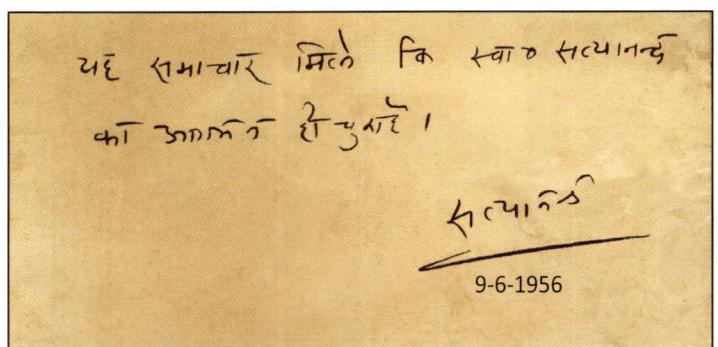

यह समाचार मिले कि स्वा॰ सत्यानन्द
का आकस्मिक देहान्त हो चुका है ।

सत्यानन्द

9-6-1956

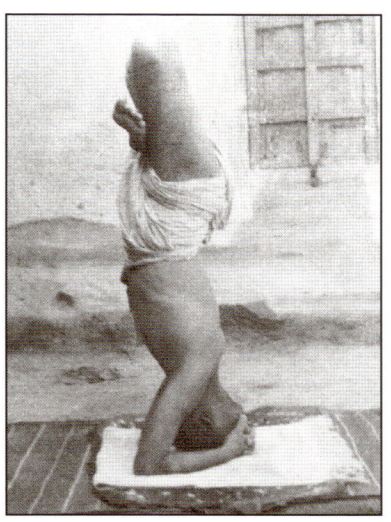

In villages of Chhattisgarh

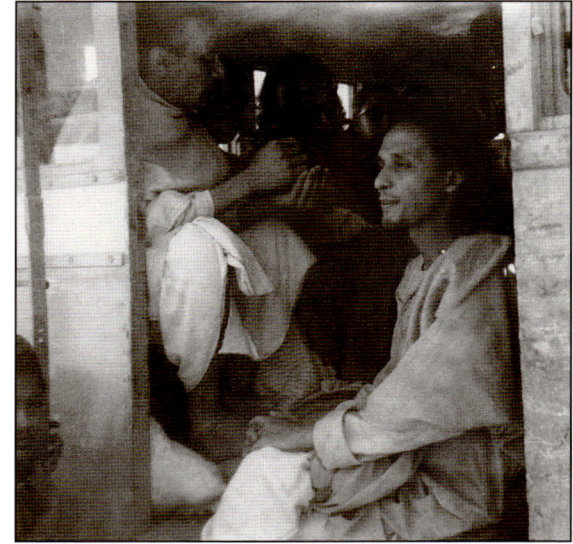

Bhagalpur, Arrah, Bihar

I am an invisible child of a thousand faces of love
That floats over the swirling sea of life,
Surrounded by the meadows of the winged shepherds,
Where stillness of divine love and beauty
Rain in the spring and bloom at midnight
Summer's warmth of softness.

Often I pass to the place
Where there is no separation of the sun and moon,
But where eternal light spreads a carpet
Of sparkling reflections of itself
Within the hearts and eyes of all,
Even those who are blind to see.
Where sweetness has no taste,
For it is the essence of all beings,
And where teardrops water flowers of happiness
And pass into brooklets of experience
And then to the open sea.

Life often cuts at my body and mind,
And though blood may be seen passing,
And a cry might be heard,
Do not be deceived that sorrow could dwell within my being,
Or suffering within my soul.
There shall never be a storm
That can wash the path from my feet,
The direction from my heart,
The light from my eyes,
Or the purpose from this life.

I know that I am untouchable to the forces
As long as I have a direction, an aim, a goal:
To serve, to love, and to give.

Strength lies in the magnification of the secret qualities
Of my own personality, my own character,
And though I am only a messenger, I am me.
Let me decorate many hearts
And paint a thousand faces with colours of inspiration
And soft, silent sounds of value.

Let me be like a child,
Run barefoot through the forest
Of laughing and crying people,
Giving flowers of imagination and wonder
That God gives free.

Do I have time to ask whom I shall love,
From whom shall I ask for something more
Than all I have been given,
Or what is meant by the signs that pass before my windows.
I learned to read half a century ago
But found it useful only for speaking
To those who continue to live by books.

I shall not pretend to understand
Nor shall I try to reason
For the satisfaction of rationalization.
Yesterday I sat in the park
And shared an orange and an afternoon
With the divines and myself.

And who am I?
Don't be deceived by my words, my manner, my way,
Or by my friendliness, or by the image of that of a man.
I sleep, eat, talk and play with you and others,
But remember that the gift of inspiration, or perfection,
Is a priceless island of treasure,
Which that whom we call God
Placed at the end of rainbows.

If I believe I have the strength
To hold back seas, to move mountains,
And the determination to live and love life,
It is because I have felt and seen an image of inspiration
Visible to my unseeing eyes.

Yes, I cried yesterday when I read sorrow
In the heart of my love,
For I am more than human,

And I laughed from my belly
When I saw two camels playing in a sea of yellow.
I am not insensitive, nor have I dulled my senses,
But never shall I become submerged or lost
In the experience of these images,
Of these feelings, of these emotions.

Don't think that as a child
My heart cannot turn as hard as stone,
When the arrow of opposition to what I believe in
Tries to pierce my centre of principle and character.
I have a cause, a meaning, a worth for individuality,
All as a means for living in this life,
For striding steps forward, for achieving a mission.

Shall I fall on bended knees
And wait for someone to bless me
With happiness and a life of golden dreams?
No. I shall run into the desert of life with my arms open,
Sometimes falling, sometimes stumbling,
But always picking myself up, a thousand times if necessary,
Sometimes happy.

Often life will burn me,
Often life will caress me tenderly
And many of my days will be haunted
With complications and obstacles,
And there will be moments so beautiful
That my soul will weep in ecstasy.
I shall be a witness,
But never shall I run or turn from life, from me.
Never shall I forsake myself
Or the timeless lessons I have taught myself,
Nor shall I let the value
Of divine inspiration and being be lost.
My rainbow-coloured bubble
Will carry me further than beyond the horizon's settings,
Forever to serve, to love, and to live
As a sannyasin.

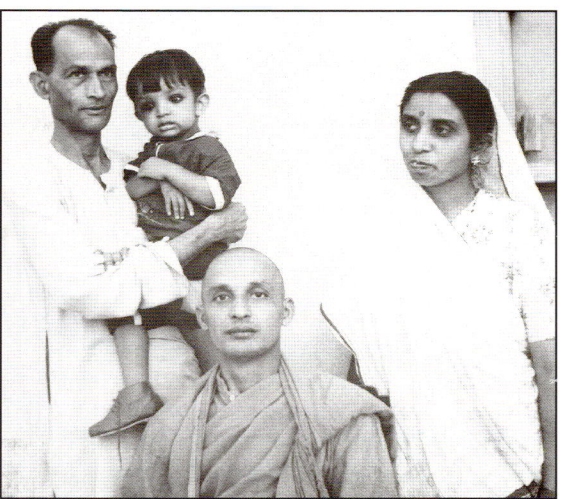

Rajnandgaon, Chhattisgarh

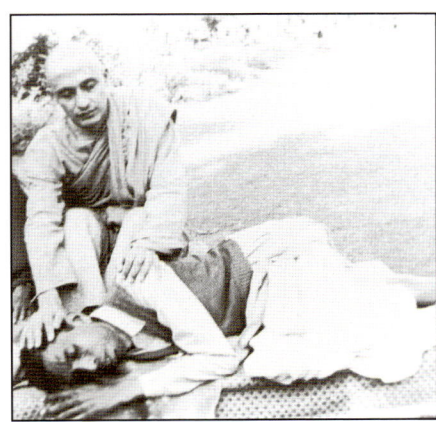

Bombay, Maharashtra

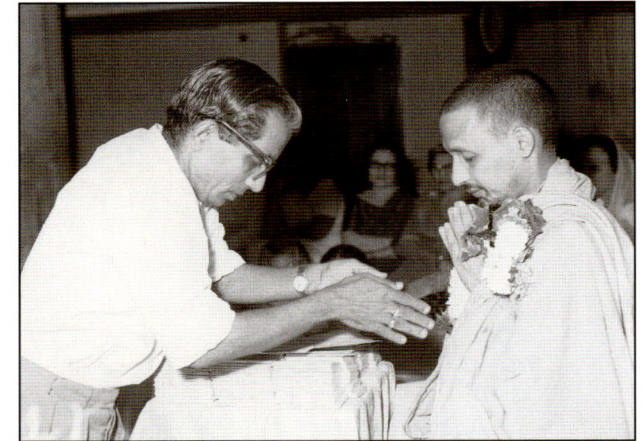

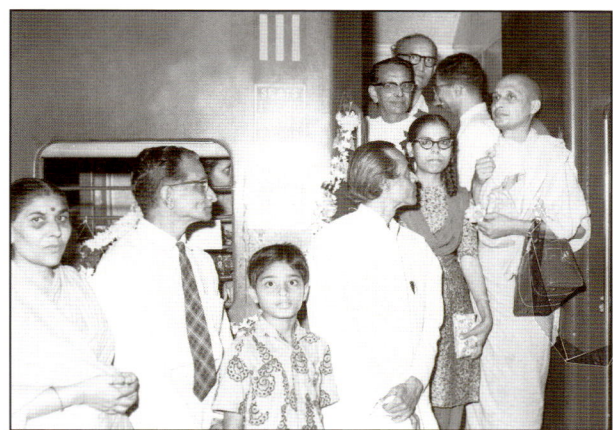

1963...

MUNGER: Karmabhoomi

Yoga is the culture of tomorrow.

Swami Satyananda

Courses at the Bihar School of Yoga, Munger, Bihar

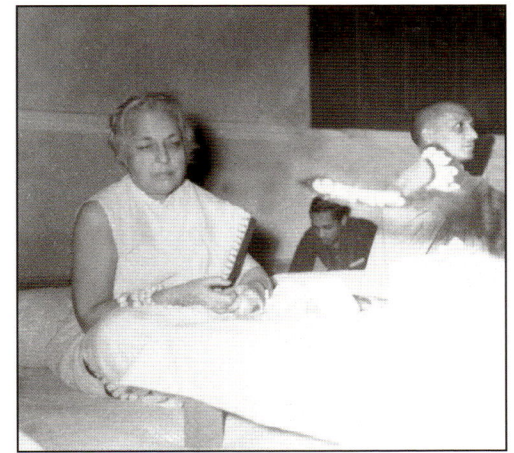

First World Yoga Convention, Munger, 1964

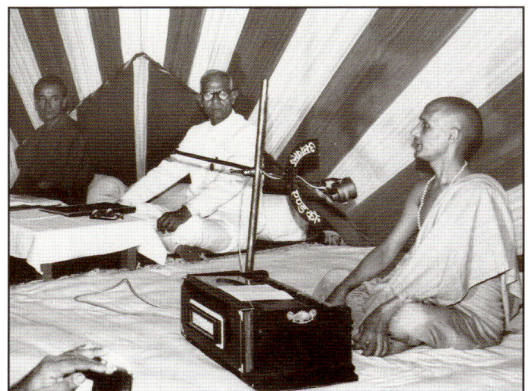

Second World Yoga Convention, Munger, 1965

Second World Yoga Convention, Munger, 1965

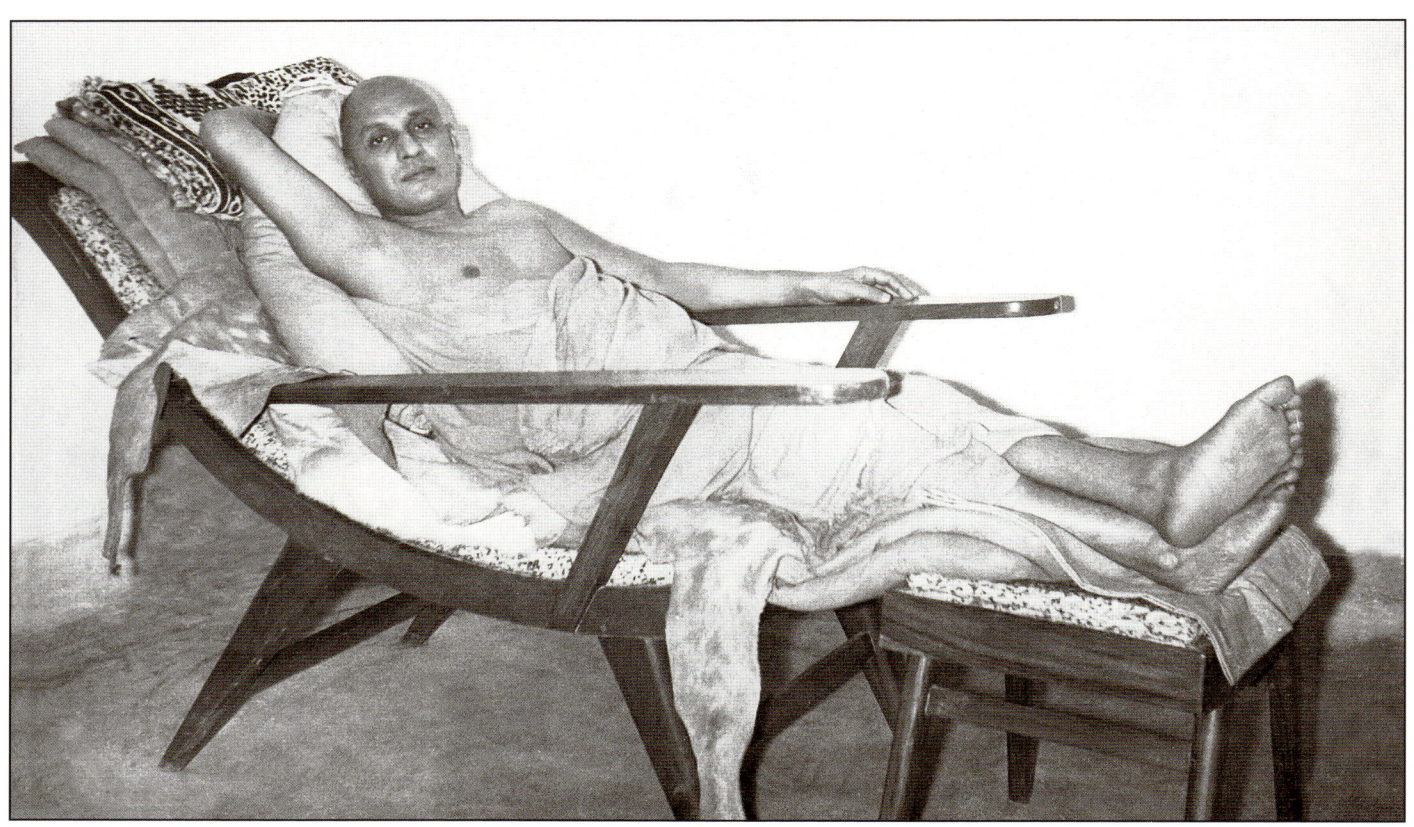

Munger, Bihar

Bombay, Maharashtra

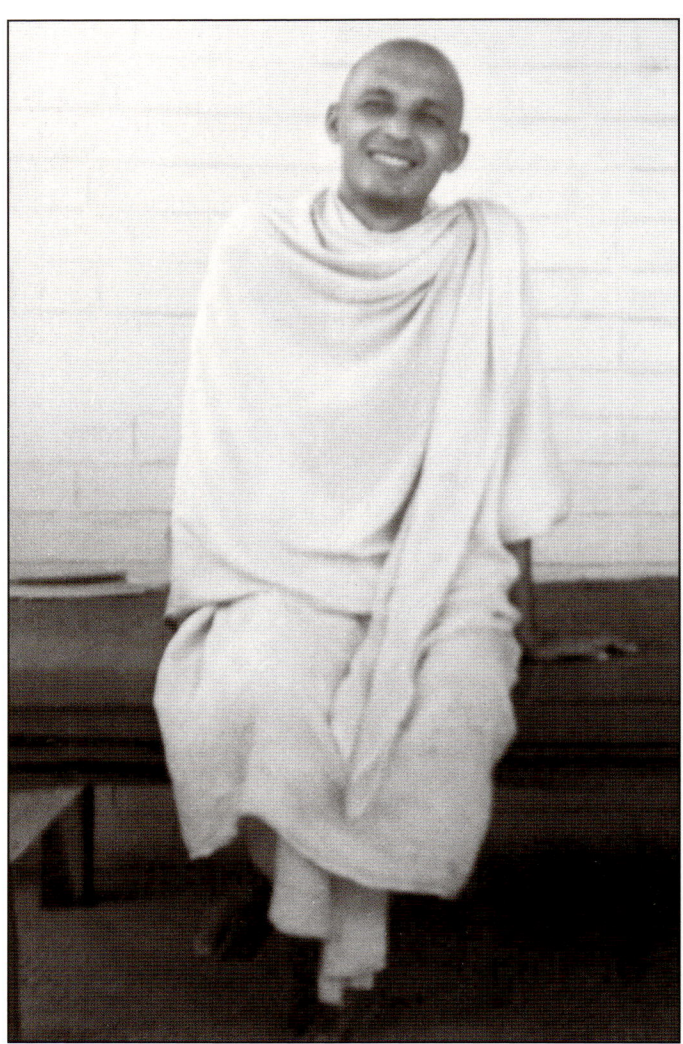

Munger, Bihar

With Shankaracharya of Sringeri Math in Munger, Bihar

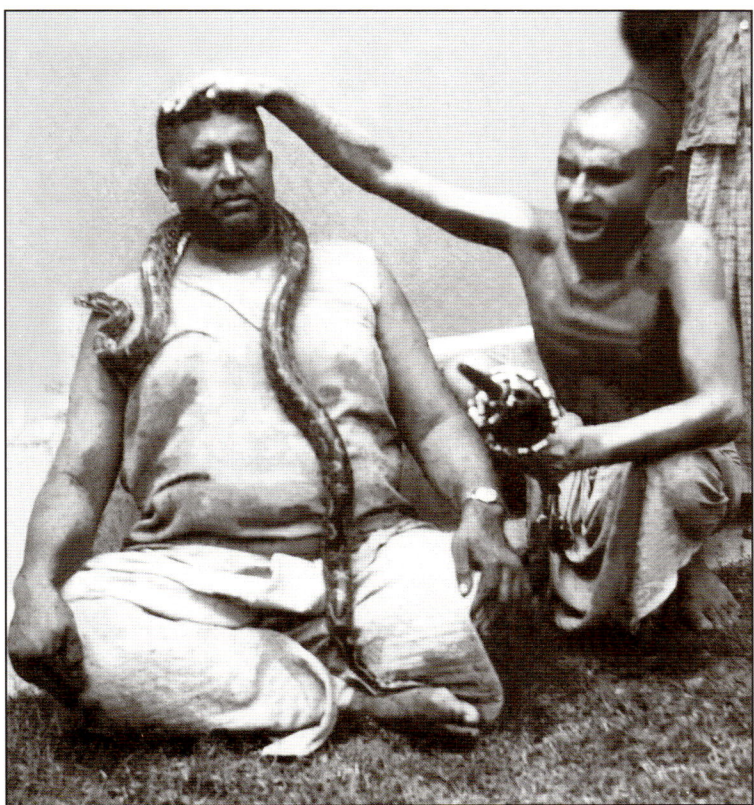

'Awakening kundalini', Munger, Bihar

Gondia, Maharashtra

Gondia, Maharashtra

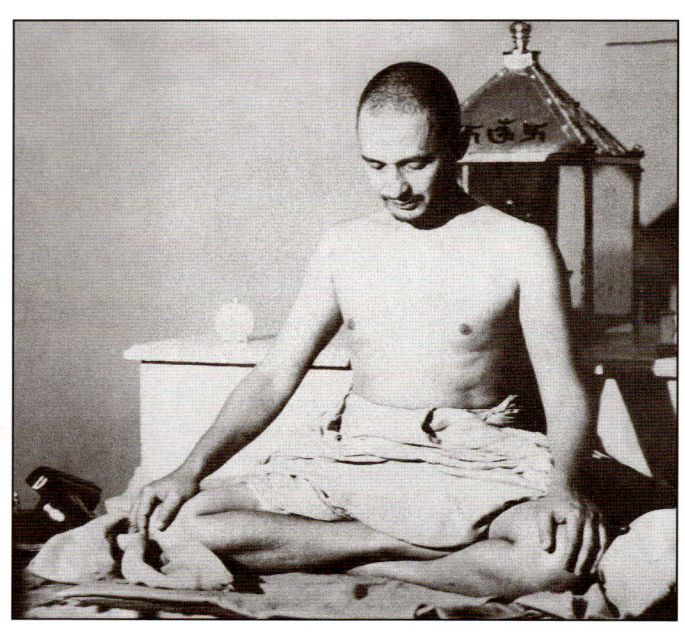

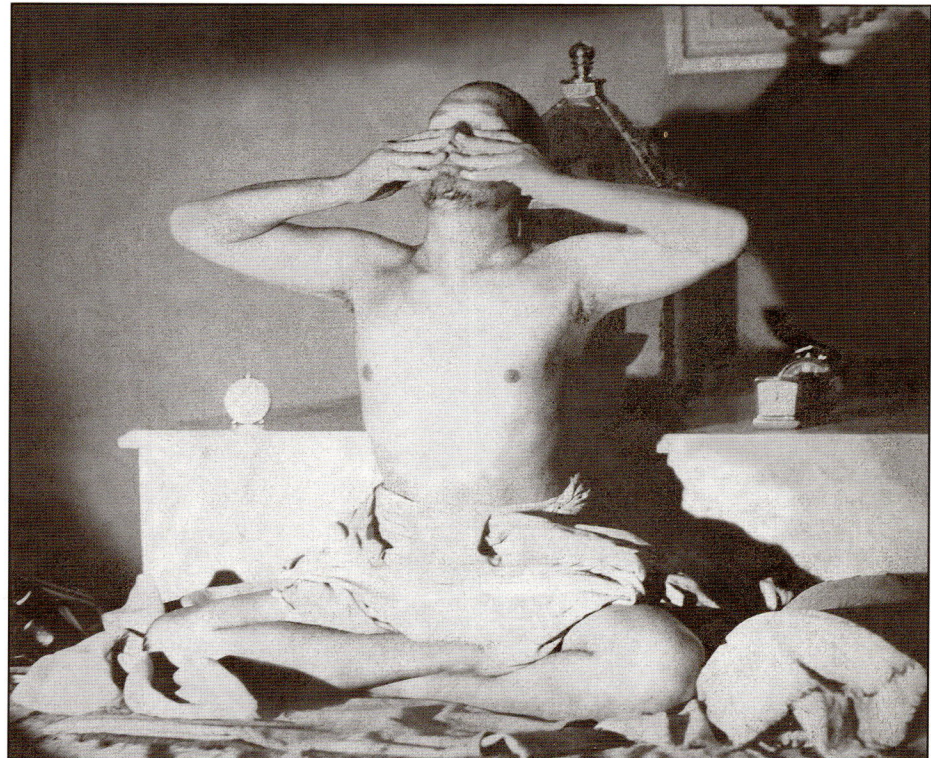

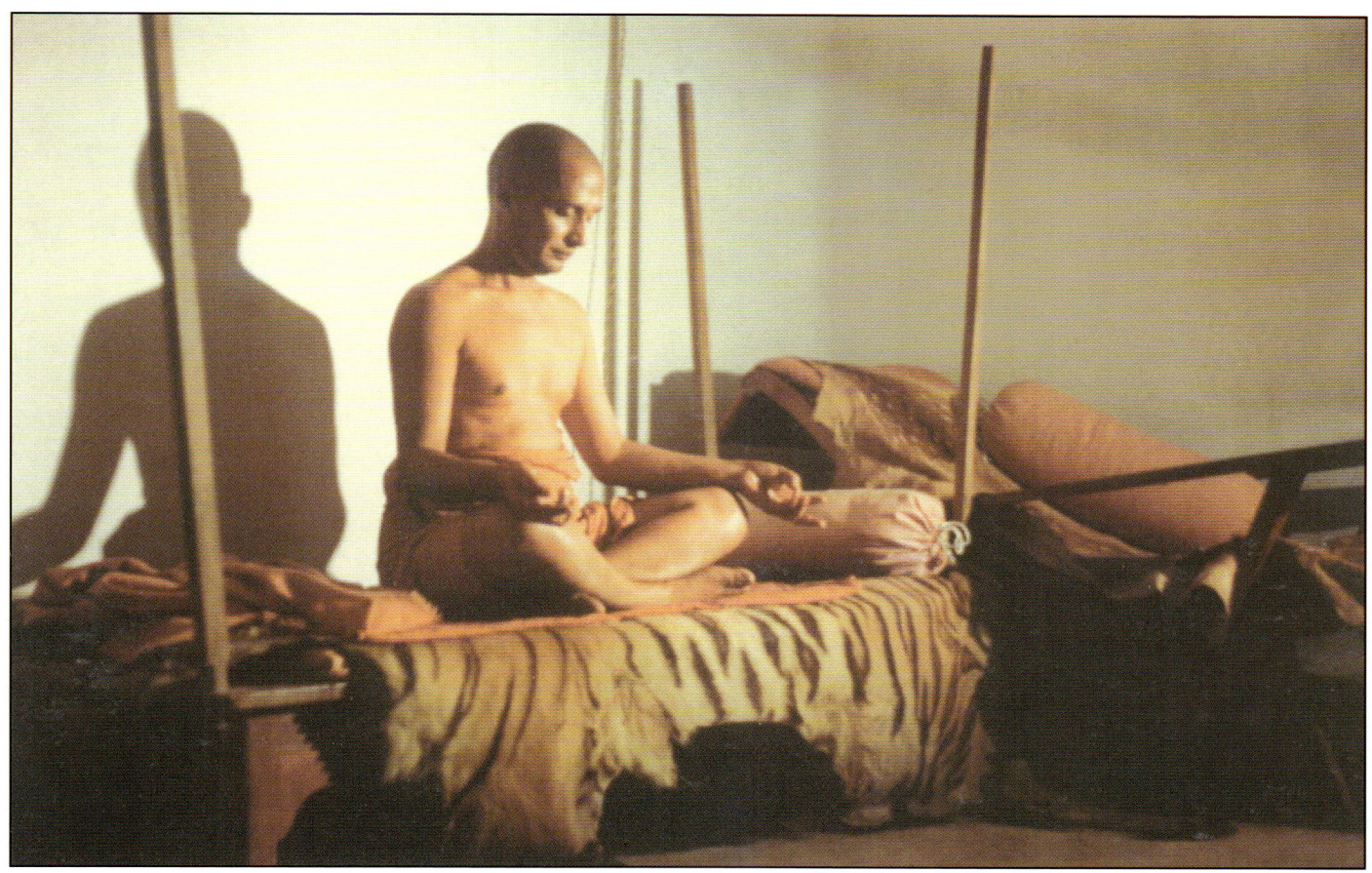

Munger, Bihar

Swami Satyananda

पंचम अन्तर्राष्ट्रीय योग सम्मेलन   FIFTH INTERNATIONAL YOGA CONVENTION
4 TO 7ᵗʰ NOV 1968

Raigarh, Chhattisgarh

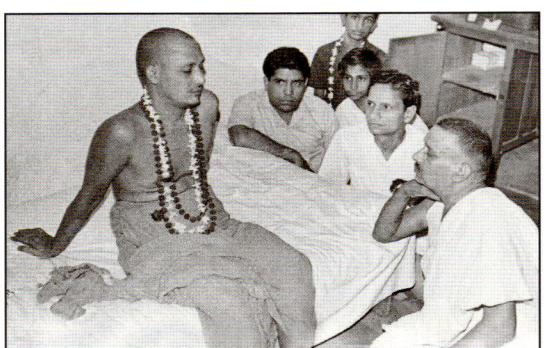

Raigarh, Chhattisgarh

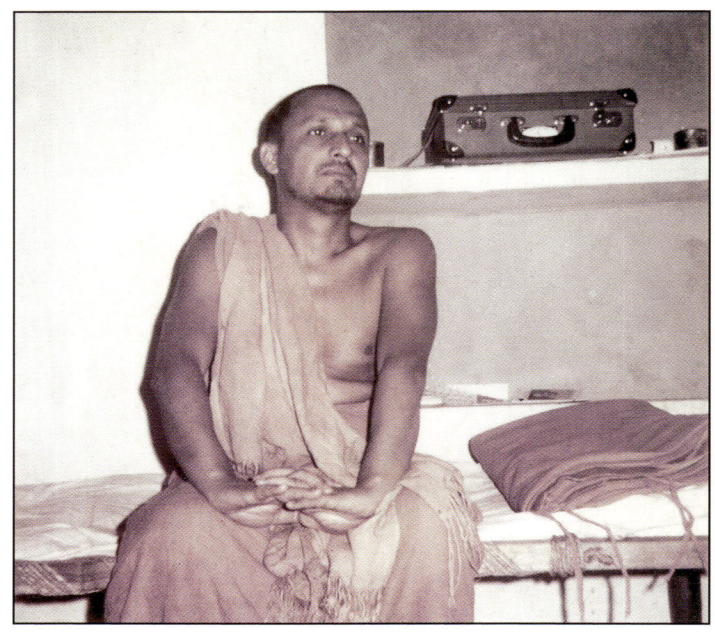

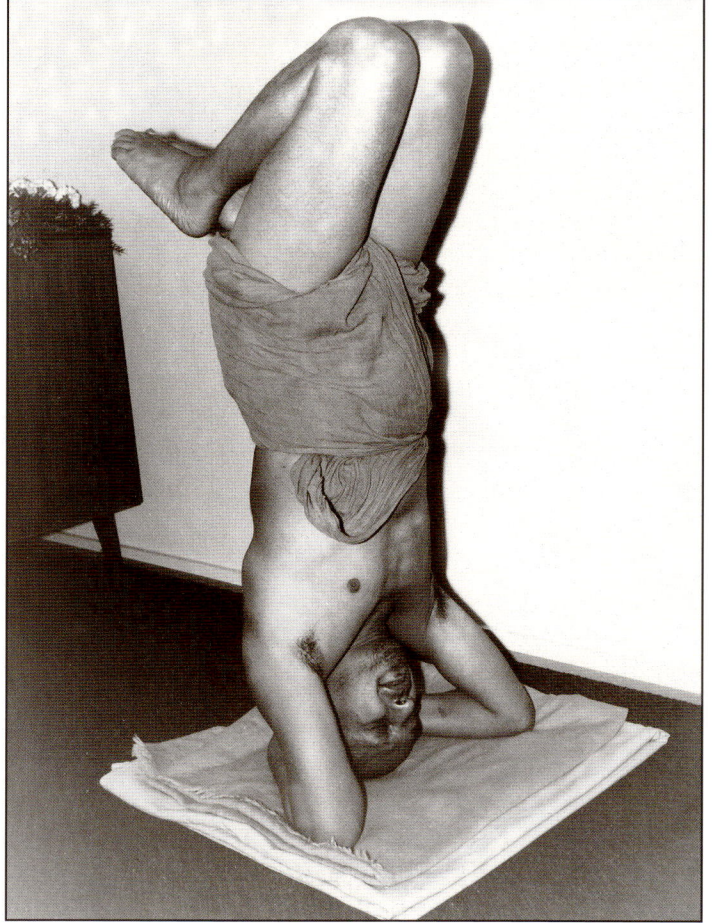

India and Germany, 1968

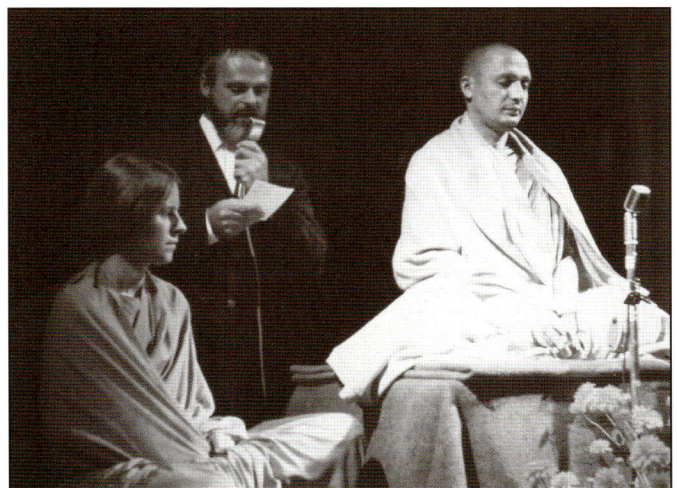

Belgium, Denmark and Switzerland, 1968

Vienna, Austria, 1968

Vienna, Austria, 1968

Paris, France, 1968

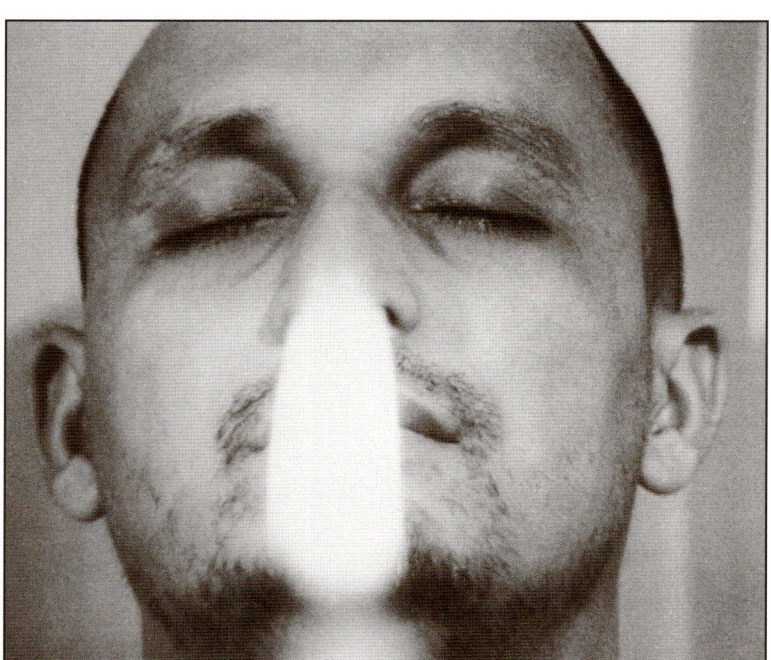

Paris, France, 1968

Westminster Abbey, London, UK, 1968

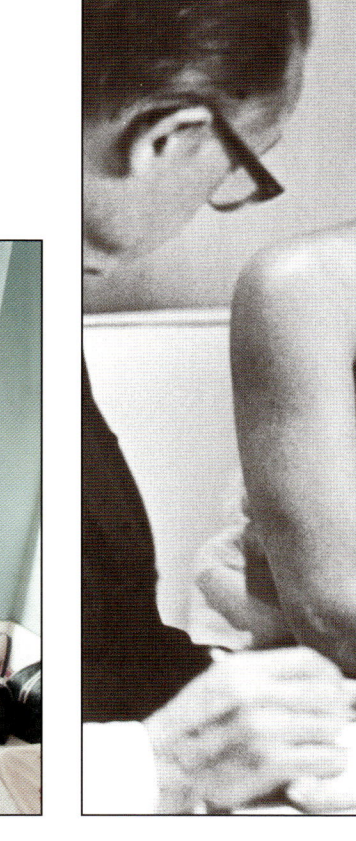

USA, 1968

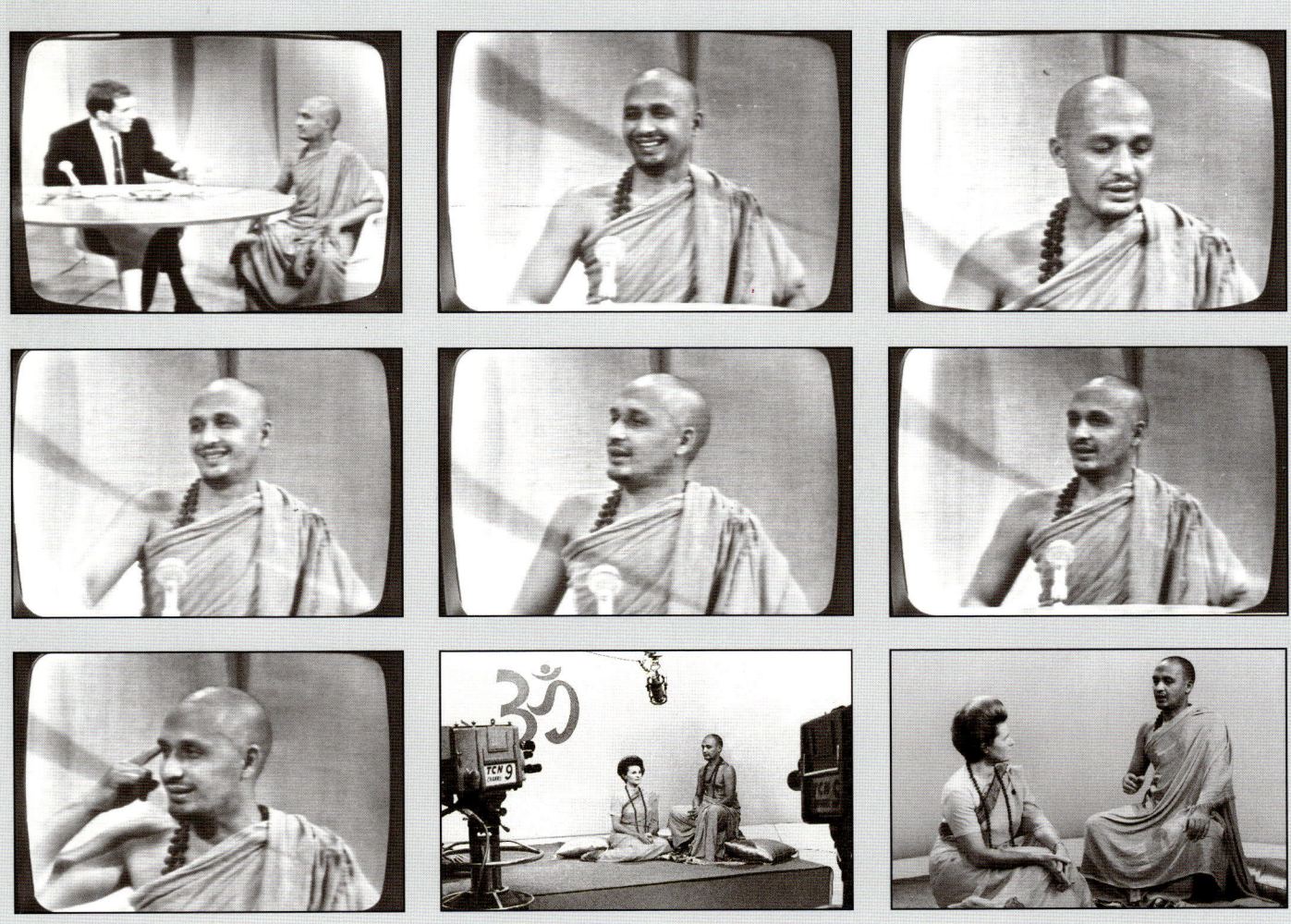

Live telecast, Australia, 1968

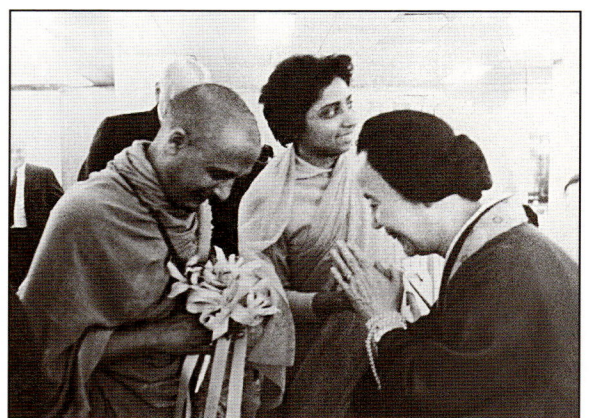

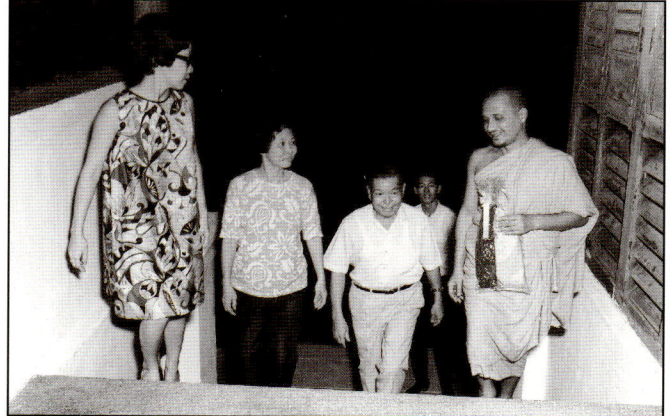

Singapore, 1968

Richmond, Australia, 1969

Munger, Bihar

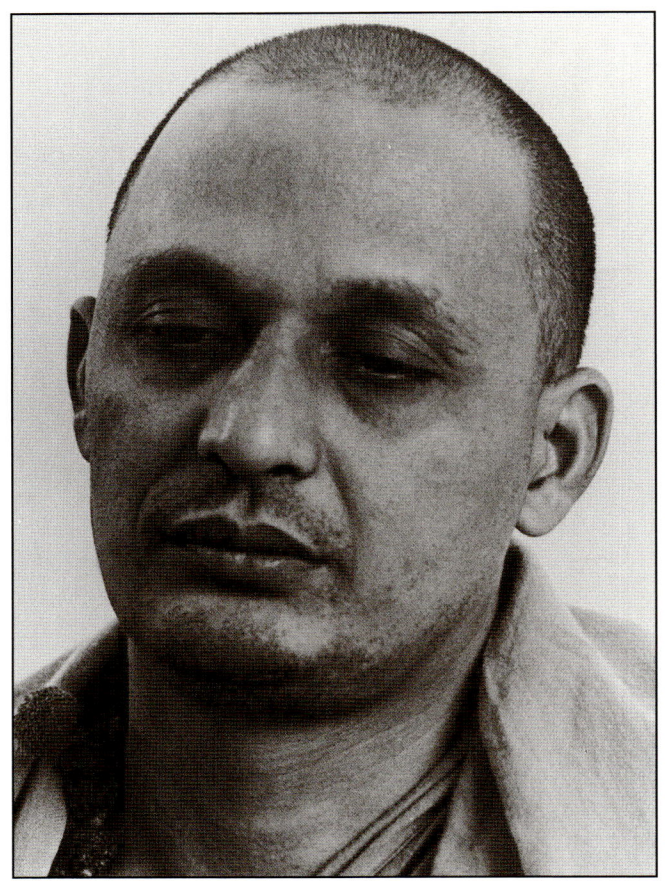
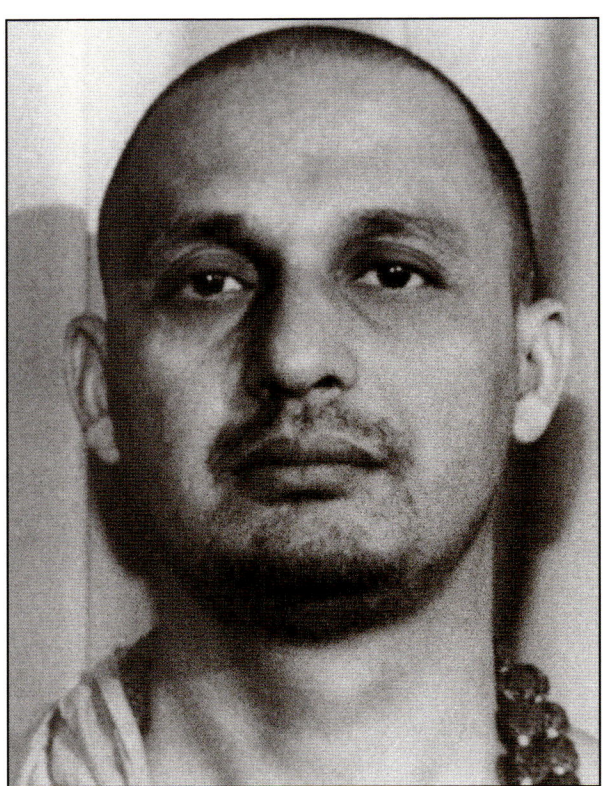

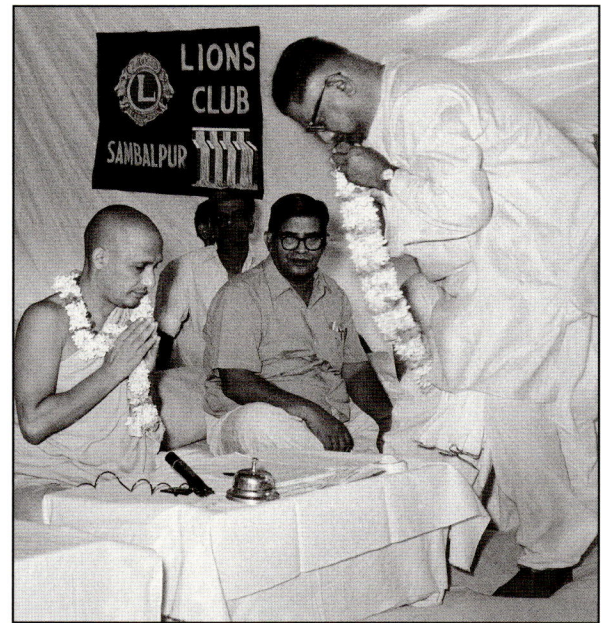

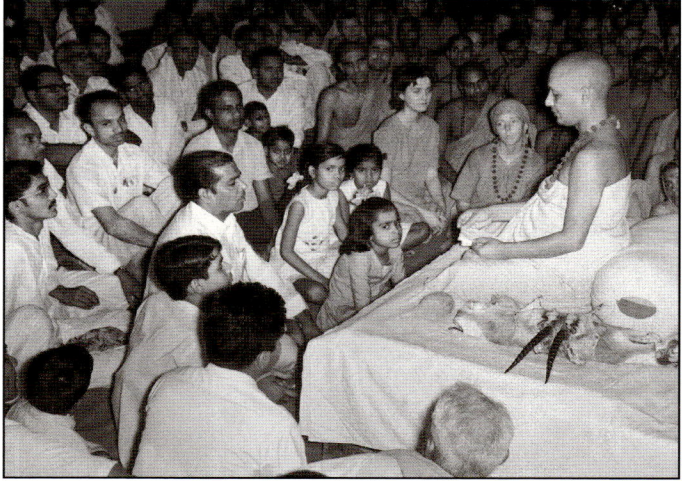

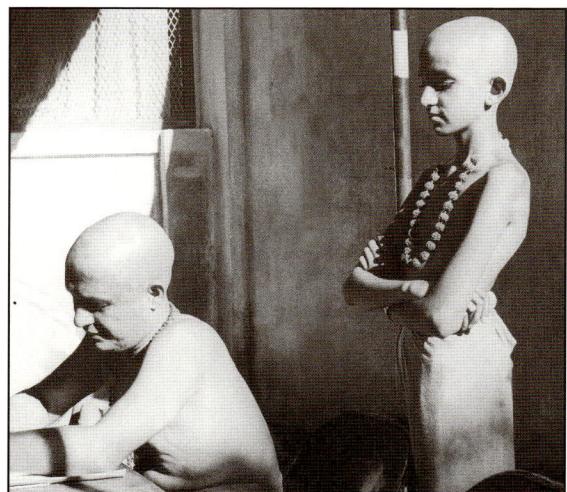

Golden Jubilee of Sri Swamiji, Munger, Bihar, 1973

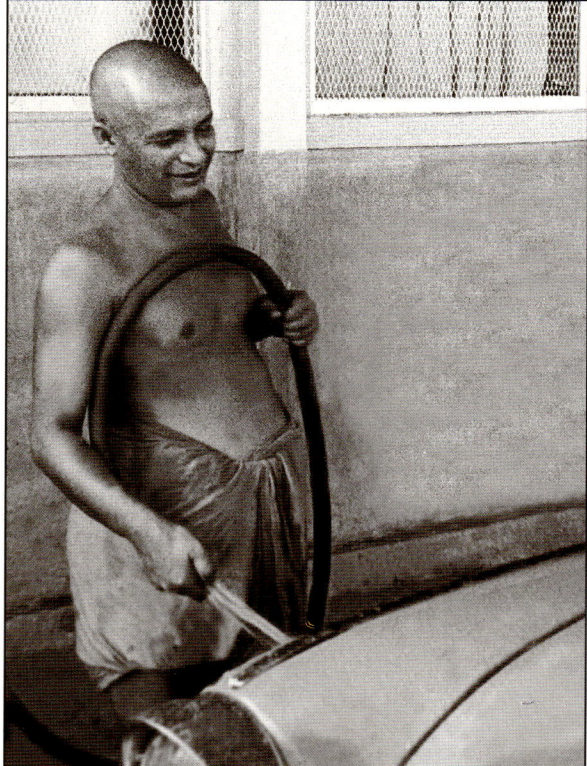

Munger, Bihar

Guru Poornima, Munger, Bihar

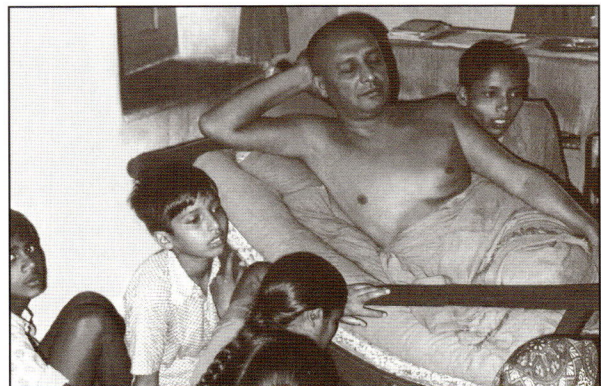

Munger, Bihar

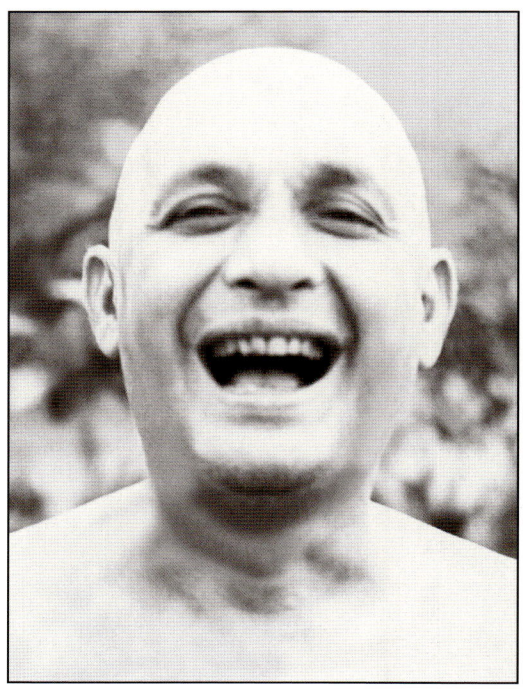

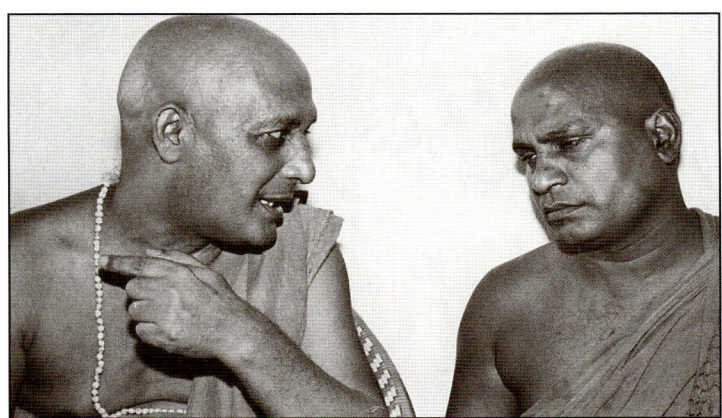

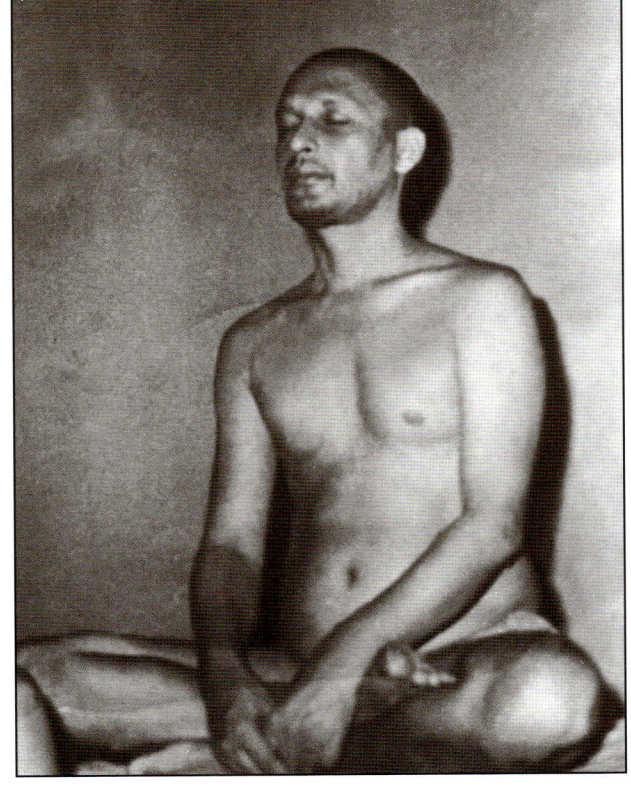

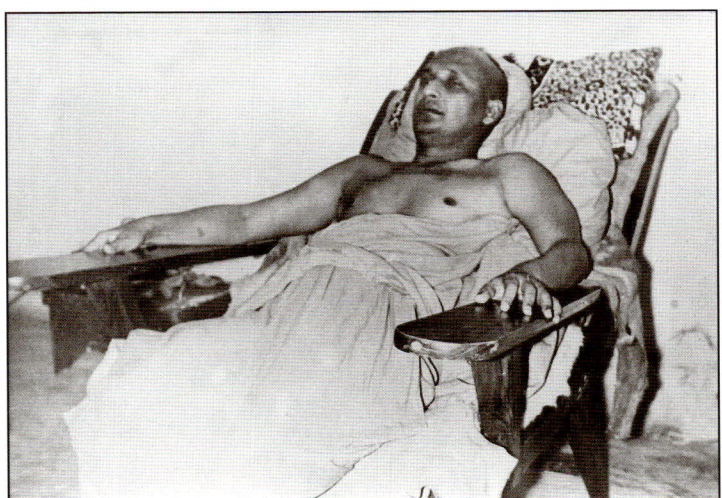

Munger, Bihar

Munger, Bihar

Bhimbandh, Bihar

Munger, Bihar

Bihar School of Yoga

Sadhana Hall

Yajnashala

Shaktipeeth

Ganga Darshan

Before

After

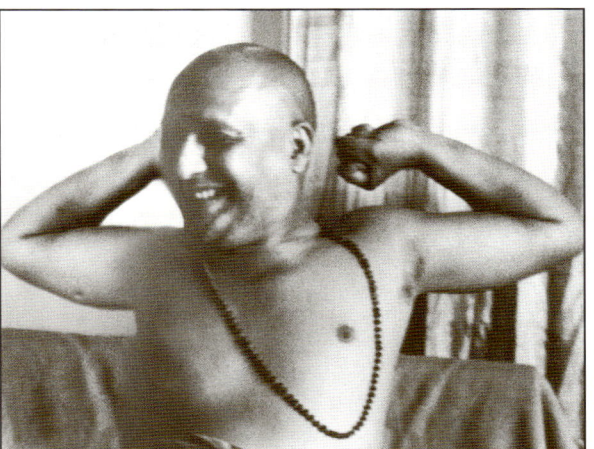

Patna, Bombay and Munger

Convención el Jubileo De Plata. De Swami

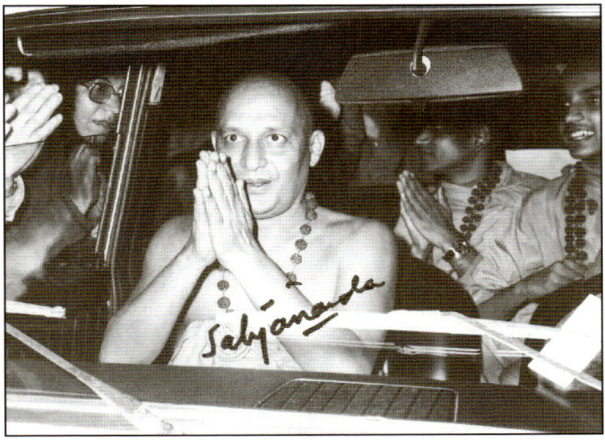

Bogota, Colombia, 1975

Newspaper reporter:
What is your greatest achivement in life?

Sri Swamiji:
Being able to stand alone on my own two feet.

Guru Poornima, Mangrove Mountain, Australia, 1977

France, Greece and Switzerland

सत्यानन्द बिहार
इस आवासीय परिसर का
शिलान्यास
परमहंस स्वामी सत्यानन्द सरस्वती
के कर कमलों द्वारा दिनांक १५ जुलाई
१९८१ को सम्पन्न हुआ। व्ही. जी. व्यास
विद्युत श्रमिक गृह निर्माण सहकारी समिति जबलपुर

Raipur, Jabalpur and Trivandrum

Thane, Maharashtra

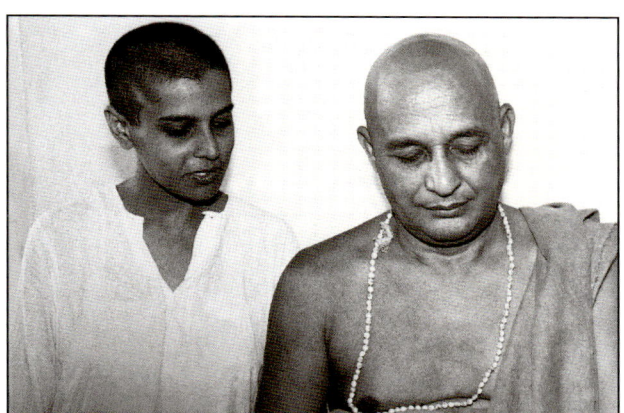

San Augustin, Colombia

San Jose, Los Angeles and Ann Arbor, USA, 1982

Ann Arbor and New York, USA, 1982

New York, Elizabeth and Washington DC, USA, 1982

151

New York, Denver and Washington DC, USA, 1982

Puerto Rico, 1982

"Return to India by 16th January, 1983."

1983...

Towards Destiny

Yoga will emerge as a mighty world culture and change the course of world events.

Swami Satyananda

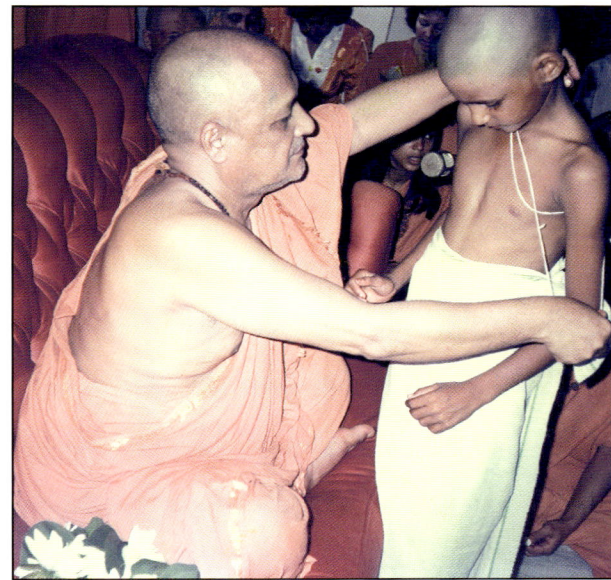

Munger, Bihar

Ganga Darshan, Munger, Bihar

Ganga Darshan, Munger, Bihar

Ganga Darshan, Munger, Bihar

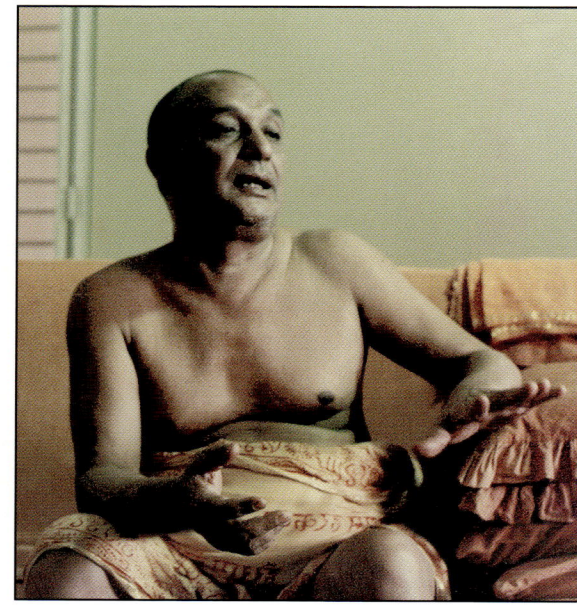

YOGA KEERTI STAMBHA

'YOGA WILL EMERGE AS A MIGHTY WORLD CULTURE AND CHANGE THE COURSE OF WORLD EVENTS'

— SWAMI SATYANANDA

England, 1984

Australia, 1984

Australia, 1984

Spain and France, 1984

Australia, 1985

Hari Om Tat Sat

There are different stages in the life of a sannyasin. First, he lives and serves the guru, then he builds an ashram and serves, then he renounces the ashram and his working place. At first he works with a limited group and then, having been united with the universal consciousness, he works to achieve a universal aim, leaving the limited group. This state is known as kshetra sannyasa.

On 8.8.88, Sri Swamiji set out alone, on foot from Ganga Darshan, Munger, to begin his long pilgrimage through the siddha tirthas of India. He took with him two dhotis, a mala and 108 rupees, the same amount he had received from Swami Sivananda when he first set out as a parivrajaka from Rishikesh in 1956, five decades earlier.

In accordance with Swami Sivananda's instructions, when Sri Swamiji started the work of spreading yoga, he had to stop the paramahamsa sadhana for some time in order to make yoga available for all. The first instruction that Sri Swamiji had received from Swami Sivananda was to serve. However, when all the inner samskaras are burnt through selfless service, then higher sadhanas begin.

In Tryambakeshwar, Sri Swamiji resumed his sadhana, which he had left while working to fulfil the mandate of spreading yoga as per his guru's instructions. Here he lived in a small room, eight by eight feet, which he cleaned and maintained himself. He slept on the floor, spreading a mat. He took only sprouted mung for lunch and brahma khichari for dinner, which he prepared himself. There was no running water or electricity in his room, he did not meet anybody. He was totally absorbed in sadhana, observing complete silence the whole day. During this period he received the inner vision of his sadhana place in Rikhia and instructions regarding the sadhana he would perform there.

Namo Narayana

Lord Vishwanath of Kashi gave me his blessings.

Vindhyvasini promised me.

Sankat Mochan, yes, I filed an application there.
Not for myself and certainly not for BSY,
but for someone, somewhere in troubled waters.

Sangam was refreshing.

Pashupatinath had an air of control and discipline.

Vaishnava Devi stirred me.

When I took a dip at Brahma Kund at Haridwar,
my whole body felt the sweetness of that drop
of nectar which the Puranas speak of.

Yamuna Devi at Yamunotri did speak to me.

Ganga at Gangotri inspired a dream.
Perhaps an impossible dream, but if she wishes,
there is nothing which I consider impossible.

Kedarnath, O Lord! Where I lost myself.
The time, the direction and all that is empirical.
I am afraid to have that experience again.

Badri Vishal, a pleasant culmination of all
the beautiful experiences of life.

And finally Sivanandashram,
words fail to describe the experience.
Was I reliving a past?
I did not feel the absence of Swamiji,
and certainly, I told him that the ashram
was a powerhouse of spiritual life.

With this I have completed the first part
of my mendicancy.

Khajuraho, 18–20 November, 1988

Khajuraho, a tribute paid to Lord Shiva by the Chandela dynasty, was a haunting experience of the rites and rituals that were an inseparable part of the lives of our ancestors: the rishis and the munis who not only gave birth to our civilization, but also dedicated their lives to the exploration of energy and consciousness behind matter.

The sublime depiction of that dramatic cosmic process of creation revealed life as a prayer. Warriors, musicians, devas, apsaras, gandharvas, men, women and beasts came alive and spoke in unison of a time when not just eroticism, as has been overly emphasized in all depictions of the temple, but every aspect of life was considered as a means to reach God.

Chitrakoot, 21 November, 1988

It was on this very spot, at the ghat of Chitrakoot, that sages gathered to watch Sant Tulsidas grinding sandalwood paste to anoint a tilak on his ishta devata, Sri Rama, and the Lord revealed himself in person. Here, amidst the sylvan setting of Kamadgiri, I delved into the time when Sri Rama eternally sanctified this soil by taking refuge there. During a few reflective moments, as I rested at the foot of the mountain where thousands do parikrama, the murmuring streams, dancing trees and flowing rivers sang to me of the glorious year when Sri Rama with Sita and Lakshmana played his lila at Chitrakoot.

In Vasukinath, as I lay under a shady tree,
I had a dream vision of a hooded serpent
coiled around my neck and the clear instruction,
"Become a Chakravarti." So I should
continue my chakram of the tirthas.

I performed the nine days of Navaratri anushthana
amidst the spiritual sanctity of Kamakhya.

On Dashami I worshipped
the Devi-incarnate kanya
and performed the ritual of washing her feet.
The purity and innocence of the shraddha
which came alive in me was that of a child
who calls out to his mother and I did receive
an answer through her.

In Kalighat, Calcutta, I had darshan of Kali,
the destroyer of kaal and destiny.

Jagannath Puri was full of ananda.
I simply transcended myself as I sat for hours
under the shaded groves in the temple precincts.
I cherish a longing
to be once again in that courtyard
where shraddha becomes a living experience.
There I met Swamis Nityabodha,
Mahatma and other Aussies.

With this the second part of my mendicancy is over.

Maihar, 22 November

The long and steep climb up to the shrine of Sharada Devi, as I rested at intervals due to footsore from my trek to Kedarnath, was reminiscent of the ascent of kundalini to sahasrara, resting and reposing at each chakra.

Sharada Devi, goddess of vidya, enshrined at sahasrara, to whom noted musicians and artists pay tribute, my salutations to you for awakening the creative energy.

Amarkantak, 3–7 December

Amarkantak, 'the forest of the immortals', vibrant with the energy of tapasvis, great rishis and munis who have practised sadhana there from time immemorial, breathed an air of tranquillity, harmony and balance. During my dip at the Narmada Udgam, I felt as if my body was being caressed by the breath of Shiva, from whose body she had emanated.

A bath at Kapil Dhara where the icy cold Narmada falls freely, a sip of water at the source of Sone, a walk through the deep forest to Bhrigu Kamandal and resting at Mai ki Bagiya, I felt oneness with nature.

Every night as my physical body rested at the ashram of the Udasin Sampradaya, my astral self was out in the open, majestically walking with Shiva, body besmeared with bhasma, snake coiled around the neck, trident and damaru in hand, stalking the wild forest.

Mahakaleshwar, Ujjain 11–14 December

The eternally sanctified city of Ujjain, which was conquered with pride by Shiva, where I performed bhasma abhisheka on Mahakaleshwar, the swayambhu jyotirlingam of Lord Shiva. The ceremony lasted one and a half hours and only a few select people were present. The rest of the day was spent in fasting and chanting mantras before Lord Mahakaleshwar. The three-foot black lingam encircled by Nagraj and set with flawless perfection on a silver yoni, thronged by hundreds of devotees, silently projecting shakti from within itself, defied all understanding and brought alive the timeless tradition of shraddha and bhakti.

Kaala Bhairava, Ujjain, 14 December

You have been consuming the madira offered to you by your ardent devotees.

Now, I offer you the intoxication which has led me through several incarnations, for this is all I have.

And with this humble offering I seek your protection while I tread through the wilderness of life.

Omkareshwar, 15–16 December

This sacred Om-shaped island on the banks of the Narmada Devi, where Adi Shankaracharya received sannyasa diksha from Guru Govindapada, and later performed the miracle of absorbing the Narmada in his kamandal, transforming faith into a living experience.

There in the cave where Shankaracharya lived, as I stood with folded hands, I heard within a voice say, "What do you seek? Ask and it shall be yours." That brought to mind the utterances of Maitreyi and Nachiketas, and in an outburst of Sanskrit I said, "Digvijay – No. Immortality – not possible. Prosperity – had plenty. Moksha – it is in me. I have come here merely to fulfil my promise which I made to you thirty years ago, to return when my work is over."

A secret passage from Shankaracharya's cave led me to the garbhagriha where the jyotirlingam of Omkareshwar stood in meditative silence amidst the chanting of the mantras. Bells were chiming, conches were blowing, and amidst this tumult, as I laid my head at the feet of Omkareshwarji, I vividly experienced that this jyotirlingam was eternally luminescent in sahasrara.

Datia, 18–19 December

The Pitambari Peeth of Shakti at whose feet saints and sages have realized the Supreme – I was returning here after thirty years to find that Sri Swamiji of Pitambari Peeth had left his physical body.

He was my third tantric guru with whom I lived for four days during my parivrajaka life, after I had served Swami Sivananda at Rishikesh. His dedication to the propagation of tantric sadhana will forever remain enshrined in my life.

With this I have completed the third part of my mendicancy.

Mathura, Vrindavan, Gokul and Barsana, 1–11 January, 1989

1989 began with a pilgrimage to Mathura Mandal or Vraj where Lord Krishna manifested as an avatara in the Dwapara Yuga and where he enacted the entire Vraj lila. The Lord himself has stated in *Varah Purana* that there is no other place in all the three worlds dearer to him than Vraj or Mathura.

The crystal blue waters of Yamunotri flow freely through this town, and sitting on its bank I delved deep into the nostalgic memories of the playful lila of Krishna with Radha, which has been lyricized by renowned poets time and again.

Everything in Vraj resounded with the blissful memories of Krishna consciousness, whether it was a darshan of Gokul, the first home of Krishna where he acquired the name 'Makhan Chor', or Vrindavan where he slaughtered Kaliya and enacted his rasa lila with the gopis, and acquired the name 'Rasiya', or a parikrama of Govardhana Parvat where he protected his people from Indra's wrath by lifting the mountain on his finger, thus acquiring the name 'Giridhara', or a stroll through Barsana where his favourite gopi, Radha, lived.

I spent twelve days in the land of Krishna at Swami Akhandanandaji's ashram, and during that time the entire Bhagavata Katha came alive with its colourful stories of a legend that will forever inspire me. It was here too that I had darshan of the great saint, Devraha Baba.

Kumbha Mela: Prayag, Allahabad, 12–14 January and 2–7 February

Prayag, the confluence of Ganga, Yamuna and Saraswati, the symbols of ida, pingala and sushumna, has been forever eulogized as the king of tirthas or Tirtharaj. The *Padma Purana* states, "Just as the sun is supreme among the planets and the moon is supreme among the stars, Prayag is the supreme tirtha." Poorna Kumbha Mela is held at Prayag every twelve years when the planetary positions of Brihaspati or Jupiter in Vrisha rashi and Surya or the sun in Makar rashi are affected. This year was especially auspicious as Somavati Amavasya took place after 172 years.

I took part in two 'Snan Parva' or bathing festivals, that of Makar Sankranti on 14th January and Somavati Amavasya on 6th February. The charged waters of Sangam electrified my whole body and I could easily feel the truth of the saying that a bath here gives a man rebirth in this life itself.

I called Swami Niranjan to be with me during this momentous occasion and to have darshan of Ganga, Yamuna and Saraswati Devi.

During the rest of the days we jostled with millions of devotees who had come like me and being amidst them was in itself a moving experience. Throngs of people from every culture, race and creed, with just one thought in mind: to bathe at Prayag, gave me the unique vision of witnessing faith in motion, and I could easily conceive the idea of that 'Faith' which is a dynamic principle and has been known to move mountains.

I also had the darshan of many sadhus and saints who had all gathered there, including Mahant Godavari of Juna Akhara, Devraha Baba, the Jagadguru Shankaracharyas and many other tapasvis and tyagis. For days afterwards and even now when I close my eyes, I can re-enact the vision of the crowds milling through the sandy bed of the Ganga and all the devas, gandharvas and apsaras gathered in the sky to witness this great spectacle.

Datia, 15 January–8 February

I took a few days off between the two Snan Parvas at the Kumbha to pay a visit to Pitambari Peeth at Datia for the anushthana of Tripura Sundari who has been enshrined there. The swamis accompanying me chanted Saundarya Lahari for the success of my anushthana.

Katni, 8–10 February

After my second bath at the Kumbha Mela, where I made the sankalpa to throw off the mantle of a guru and don the robes of a parivrajaka, I travelled to Katni at the invitation of Sri Agrawal to inaugurate his yoga school. Although I have totally abandoned preaching, teaching and initiating disciples, I kept this appointment as I had already committed myself earlier.

Dwarka, 18–20 February

The land where Lord Krishna migrated from Mathura with the entire Vrishni clan to set up his kingdom and enact yet another episode of his lila for which he was given the title 'Ranchhornathji', or one who fled from the battleground.

The images of Bal Gopal and Kanhaiya are replaced by that of Dwarkanath, or 'King of Dwarka'. Sitting on the banks of the Gomati river, I relived the era when the city of Dwarka which is now submerged, flourished as a kingdom of the Lord. Amidst the chanting of folk songs I had the darshan of the Chaturbhuj image of Ranchornathji glamorously decorated with 108 different types of bhoga, yet another aspect of the Divine.

My stay at Dwarka was rendered in three hours, from 7.15 to 10.15 pm. The temple doors were closed during this time so as to not disturb the Lord, and sitting in my hotel room I lost myself in *naam smaran,* remembrance of the Name, and a deep inner vision of Vishnu reposing on an eclipsed moon.

Somnath, 21–23 February

Somnath, one of the dwadash jyotirlingas, having a history which fades into legend, is said to have been originally built out of gold by Somraj, the moon god himself. Today, despite the repeated raids and ravages of destruction that the temple has faced, a stone jyotirlinga majestically glows in the temple precincts. I spent my days at the seashore in reflection and chintan.

Shirdi, 12–14 March

The samadhi of Sai Baba who has been heralded as an avatara was the first tirtha I visited in Maharashtra. It is said that not just the temple, but the entire town of Shirdi resonates with the spiritual vibrations of the great saint, Sai Baba.

Sitting at the eternally lit dhuni of Baba, I did feel a strong spiritual energy field which could only have been created by the tapasya and vairagya of a maha purusha. The early morning arati which I attended was filled with the shraddha and love of thousands of devotees who had gathered there.

Mahabaleshwar, 5–8 April
Beautifully housed in a temple of black slab stone, the jyotirlinga of Mahabaleshwar is also said to be the source of five rivers: Savitri, Krishna, Venya, Koyan and Gayatri. As a result, this jyotirlinga, which bears the mark of a Rudraksha Akara, is continually bathed by the sanctified water of these rivers.

It is said that Brahma, Mahesh and Vishnu are eternally present here and the stark beauty of the valleys, the shady and dense forests, the streams, all lend probability to this belief. I spent many hours here walking through the forests which are beautiful but sinister, and few dare to venture there. I saw the spot where Brahma held a yajna and one day I accidentally came across an abandoned Shiva temple overlooking the beautiful Krishna valley.

Tryambakeshwar, Nasik, 12–14 April
My next tirtha was to the holy cities of Nasik and Tryambakeshwar where Godavari, one of the seven holy rivers of India, originates. It was here in the Panchavati that Sri Rama spent eleven years in exile and it was here too that Sita was abducted by Ravana.

After archana at Kushravat, the source of Godavari, I had darshan of the jyotirlinga of Lord Tryambakeshwar, which is unique on account of three lingas emerging out of a single stone. Here I conducted a special pooja with chants of *Rudrashtakam*. Later I did parikrama of the mandir and had darshan of many mahatmas residing there.

Bhimashankar, 5–6 May
A pilgrimage to Bhimashankar was like a journey back to nature. The lush green forests of Bhimashankar, unspoiled and untarnished by modern civilization, radiated peace and harmony. Surrounded by hills where the rakshasi Dakini is known to reside, is the jyotirlinga of Bhimashankar. The temple itself is very ancient and, unlike other tirthas where one has to ascend to worship the deity, here the devotee has to descend a flight of steps before having darshan of the jyotirlinga.

Although this place is less known among the jyotirlingas, the tranquil setting and the spiritual vibrations make it an important tirtha. Shiva is known to have rested here after slaying the demon Tripurasura.

Ghushmeshwar, 7–9 May
Named after a bhakta called 'Ghushma', the jyotirlinga at Ghushmeshwar was a boon she received from Shiva for her unflinching devotion. It is also known as Shivalaya, because Shiva promised her that he would be eternally present here. Near this temple are the famed Ellora caves which I also visited after many years. The beautiful sculptures carved out of gigantic mountains spread over an area of one mile are breathtaking and a soothing sight for the eyes.

Nathdwara, 15–17 May

The seat of the Vallabh Sampradaya, renowned for the rites and rituals adopted by the Pushti Margis, Nathdwara gives one the feeling of actually being in the presence of Lord Krishna. The rich folklore which recounts the legend of Lord Krishna is sung daily in the courtyard which houses the deity, while devoted pujaris tend to every need of the Lord, such as bathing, dressing, eating and even fanning him while he reposes on his silken bed. Devotees are even given darshan of the decorative headgear, jewellery and the costumes of Lord Krishna amidst showers of cool water sprinkled with khas and rose fragrance, a wonderful experience for a bhakta.

According to legend, the black stone image of Sri Nathji was brought here from Mathura in 1669 and, when an attempt was later made to move the image, the wagon carrying the deity sank into the ground up to the axles, indicating that the image preferred to stay where it was.

Kankroli, 15–17 May

A little further down from Nathdwara is another important seat of the Pushti Margi sect which houses an image of Dwarkadheesh. It is a simple temple with the same elaborate ceremonies as Nathdwara. I saw here for the first time a painting which speaks of an incident when Sri Krishna received the prasad of bhang from Lord Shiva. Strangely enough, the charanamrit given to me here was thandai with bhang. I sat in the temple precincts for many hours amidst the chanting of Krishna bhajans in the local dialect.

Eklingi, 15–17 May

The temple of Eklingi is spread over a vast area and houses images of almost every deity. The main deity in the garbhagriha is that of a four-faced image of Shiva emerging from a black marble Shivalingam. The deity is elaborately decorated every day and mantras are chanted as part of the ritual. To enter the garbhagriha I was given a special robe by the pujari and had personal darshan of Eklingi Maharaj.

Pushkar, 18–20 May

Just as Prayag is known as king of tirthas, Pushkar is renowned as the guru of all tirthas. No pilgrimage is complete without a visit here. Its main importance lies in the fact that the only Brahma temple in India is found here. It is said that Rishi Agastya had his ashram here. After a dip in the Pushkar lake and a bath at Agastyakund, I had darshan of Brahmaji and conducted a special pooja at the beautiful temple.

Mount Abu, May

In the artistic and majestic Jain temple of Dilwara I meditated in front of the big dark statue of Lord Mahavir. Here I was inspired to further walk the path of self-discovery, filled with renunciation, *tyaga bhava*.

I had darshan of the cave and the place of austerity of Lord Dattatreya, which is now under the patronage of Niranjani Akhara. I had stayed here in my previous wanderings many, many years ago. I feel that my future is being directed by Lord Dattatreya.

Ajmer, May

After my time at Pushkar, I went to the Dargah of Khwaja Moinuddin Chisti and offered a chadar. Thousands come to this place to pray, forgetting their caste and religion. In that atmosphere filled with devotion and faith, I did japa and dhyana.

Gangotri and Badrinath, 30 May–20 June

This lap of my tirtha was terminated by a visit to Rishikesh, my guru's ashram, Gangotri and Badrinath. I called Swami Niranjan to accompany me on this trip. There I met many saints and mahatmas, and bathed in the icy cold waters of Ganga at Gangotri and the steaming hot water of the Tapt Kund at Badrinath. At Badrinath I also had darshan of Saraswati Udgam at Manas where she emerges with full force out of the mountain: a sight to behold!

Tryambakeshwar, 14 July

I am at Tryambakeshwar, the jyotirlinga of Lord Shiva, after twenty-six years. It was here in 1963 that the chapter of my life which led me to Munger and the propagation of yoga was first revealed to me. It was here that I made a *sankalpa,* or promise, to return and seek further enlightenment, renouncing all I achieve or accomplish in the propagation of yoga.

This morning I went to have darshan of Lord Mrityunjaya and sought his permission to spend two months of chaturmas here. A strange coincidence brings me back after so many years to the same place. His Holiness Mahant Shivgiriji Maharaj, the chief of Juna Akhara at Tryambakeshwar, invited me to stay at Neel Parvat, the very same place where I had stayed twenty-six years ago. I have chosen to stay in a goshala at the foot of Neel Parvat, a small room eight foot by eight foot, representing everything ancient in structure, purity and simplicity.

I am alone. What shall I do here? All around me rise the Brahmagiri hills from which the Godavari descends and flows on to the eastern sea. While I meditate under the gular tree outside my kutir and await His next command, I am inspired and intoxicated by the wondrous beauty of these Shivalinga-shaped mountains on all sides.

Tryambakeshwar, 18 July

Guru Poornima vrat begins today. At midnight I was bathing in the light when a cyclonic storm started and the command was clear: "Perfect the unbroken awareness of your guru mantra with every breath and beat of your heart. That is your mission now."

So here begins the next chapter of my life. And just as I gave my whole self to the accomplishment of His previous command, I shall also plunge deep into all that is required of me to perfect my new mission. The past is dead and gone. Human as I am, I may travel back into the past and circumstances may compel me to accept associations with those with whom I had interacted before, that too is His will, but my personal endeavour will be to break away from the past and fulfil the mission given to me by Lord Mrityunjaya.

Tryambakeshwar, 8 September

A question which has been haunting my mind from time to time is answered today. Where do I fulfil my next mission? Many places were offered to me, a beautiful cave at Gangotri on the banks of the Ganga, a kutir at Kedarnath and many others, but I had reserved my decision until the direction was made clear to me. I woke up at midnight as usual. The sky was quiet, the translucent rays of Ashtami were shining through the small windows of my kutir, and I found that I was once again enveloped by a strange light. The command was clear, "Go to my cremation ground, the shmashan bhoomi."

That very morning while I was boiling my tea, Swami Satyasangananda arrived all the way from Munger and the first instruction I gave her was to find the place for me. I gave her a glimpse of what I had seen and described its setting and surrounding topography. She left barely three hours after her arrival in search of the place of my description.

Tryambakeshwar, 12 September

On this day forty-three years ago, I shed all that belonged to my purvashram, the name, caste, gotra and many more things, including coat and pants, to don the geru robes. It was on this day, at Rishikesh by the banks of the Ganga, that my guru Swami Sivanandaji gave me paramahamsa diksha of the Dashnami sannyasa order.

Swami Gyanprakash arrived by mid-afternoon to inform me that barely two days after her departure, Swami Satsangi had located the exact setting in Lord Shiva's shmashan bhoomi for my further mission. That evening I performed the poornahuti for the fulfilment of my prayers, and the revelation of a divine place and a clear-cut path, just as BSY and Ganga Darshan had been revealed to me twenty-five years ago in the same place by the same Lord Mrityunjaya.

I now wish to make it clear to all of you associated with me in the past that I am dead and will continue to live in the shmashan bhoomi of my ishta devata until he has some other command for me. Prior to my final settling I will pay a visit to Kamakhya and worship Her in Her physical form which I had promised on Vijaya Dashami last year.

The hamsa has flown away
Soaring with its wings spread
Across the infinite sky.
It is searching for its ultimate abode
Since many yugas.
Knowledge it has received in abundance
From the jnanis of the world,
Grace and blessings from the Divine too.
Still today it is restlessly flapping
Its wings in search.
Looking down at its own creation
Of the three worlds
Etched across the horizon,
Yes, it is flying high
And flying ceaselessly in search,
Witnessing the world down below as lila
Alone, all alone, in the infinite sky
My soul is flying to unite with its beloved.

1989...

RIKHIAPEETH: Tapobhoomi

तुमने मुझे अनपेक्षित वरदान दिये,
अब कुछ नहीं चाहिये।

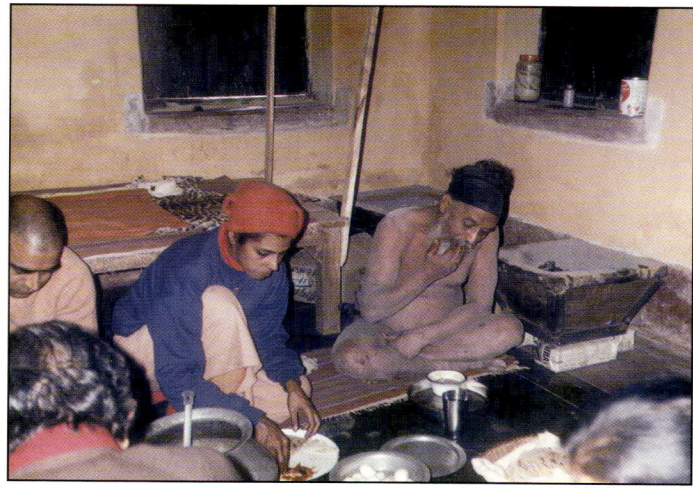

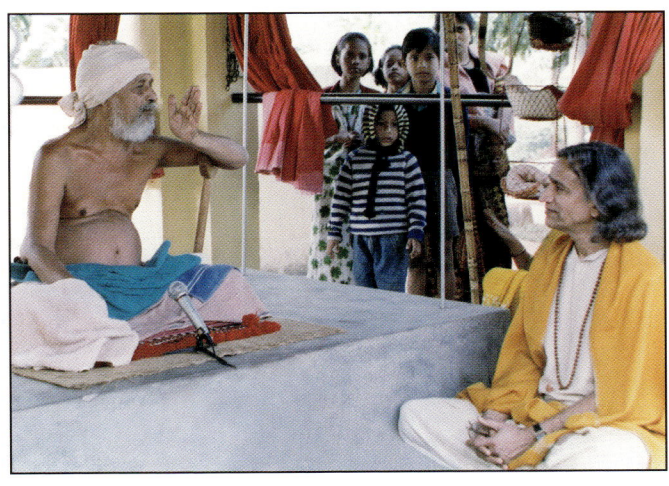

Om Namo Narayana
O Lord Mrityunjaya!
I have worshipped you
As Kaala Bhairava with one tattwa,
As Kamakshi with five tattwas,
As Vishnu with flowers, fruits, water and milk.

In many forms, in many ways
And in many places
I have worshipped whatever form
You have revealed to me as your own image.

And now, at your burial ground
I will worship you with every breath.

This I promise.

Swami Satyanand

(Navaratri, 30 September 1989)

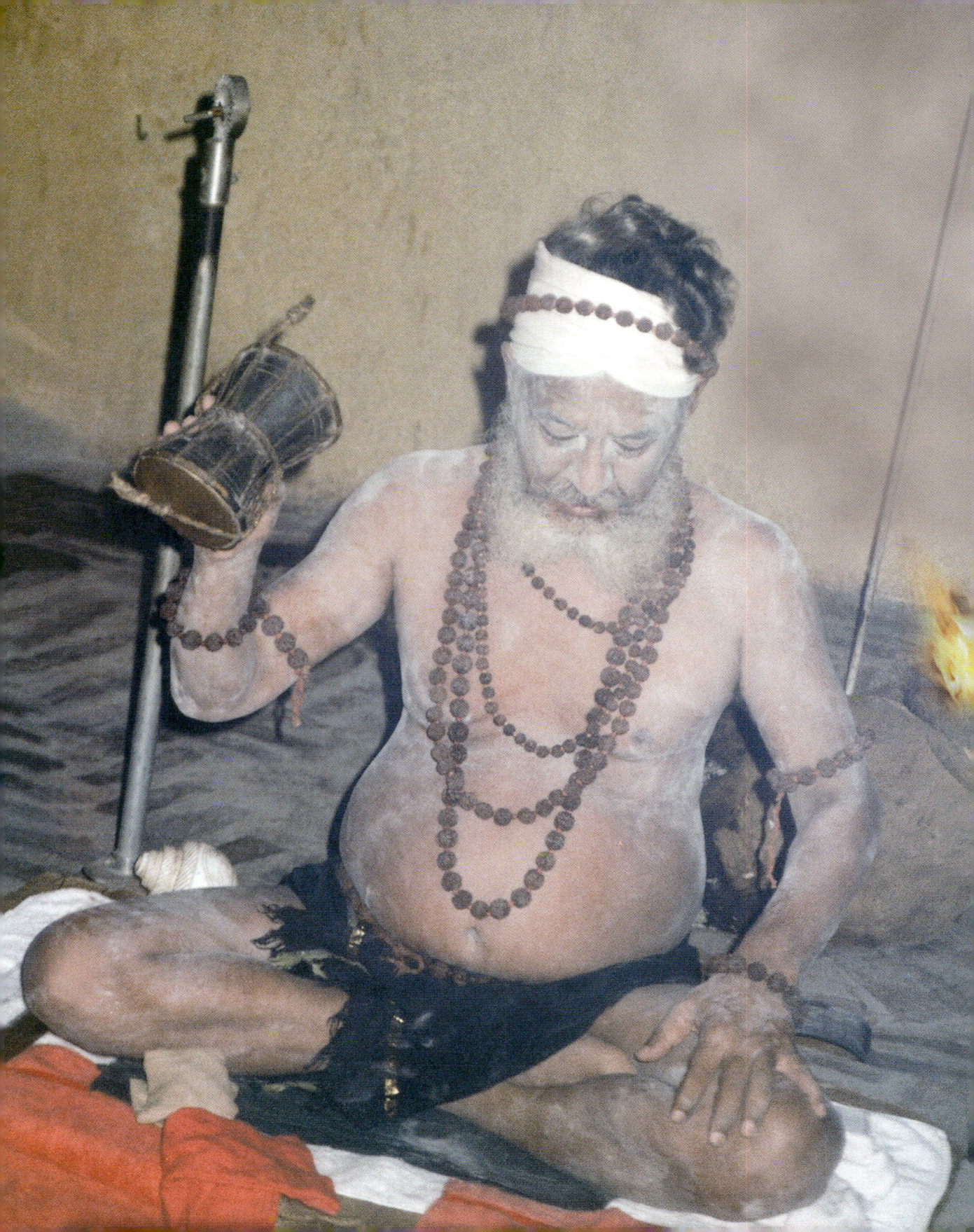

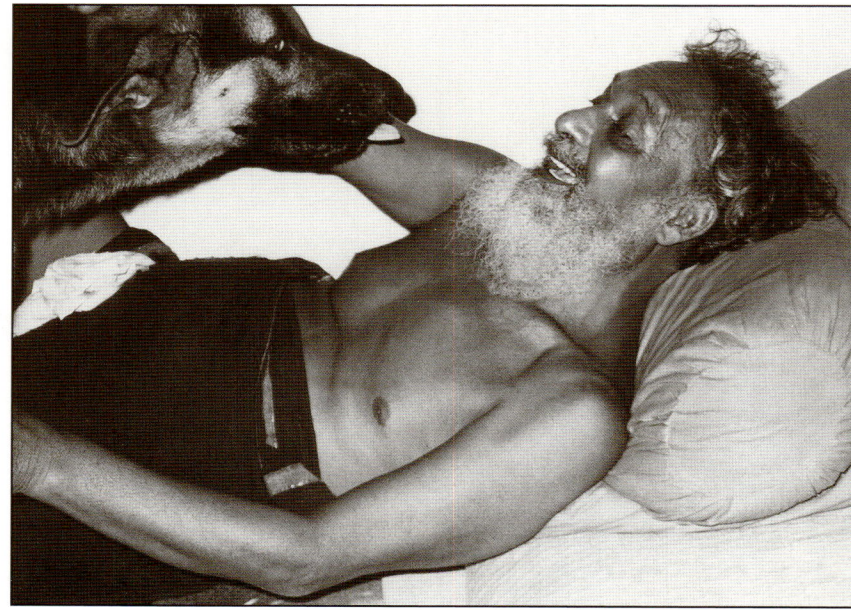

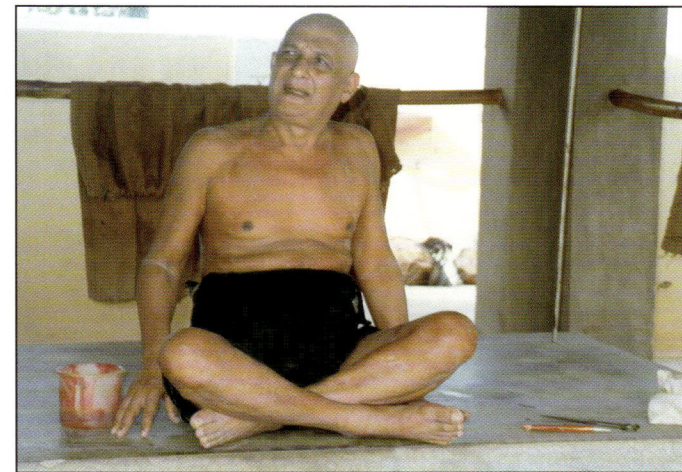

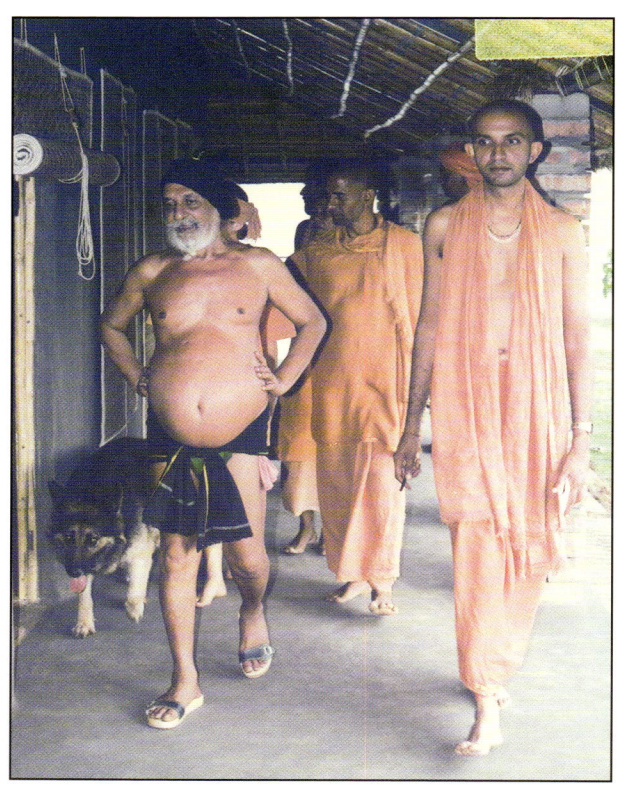

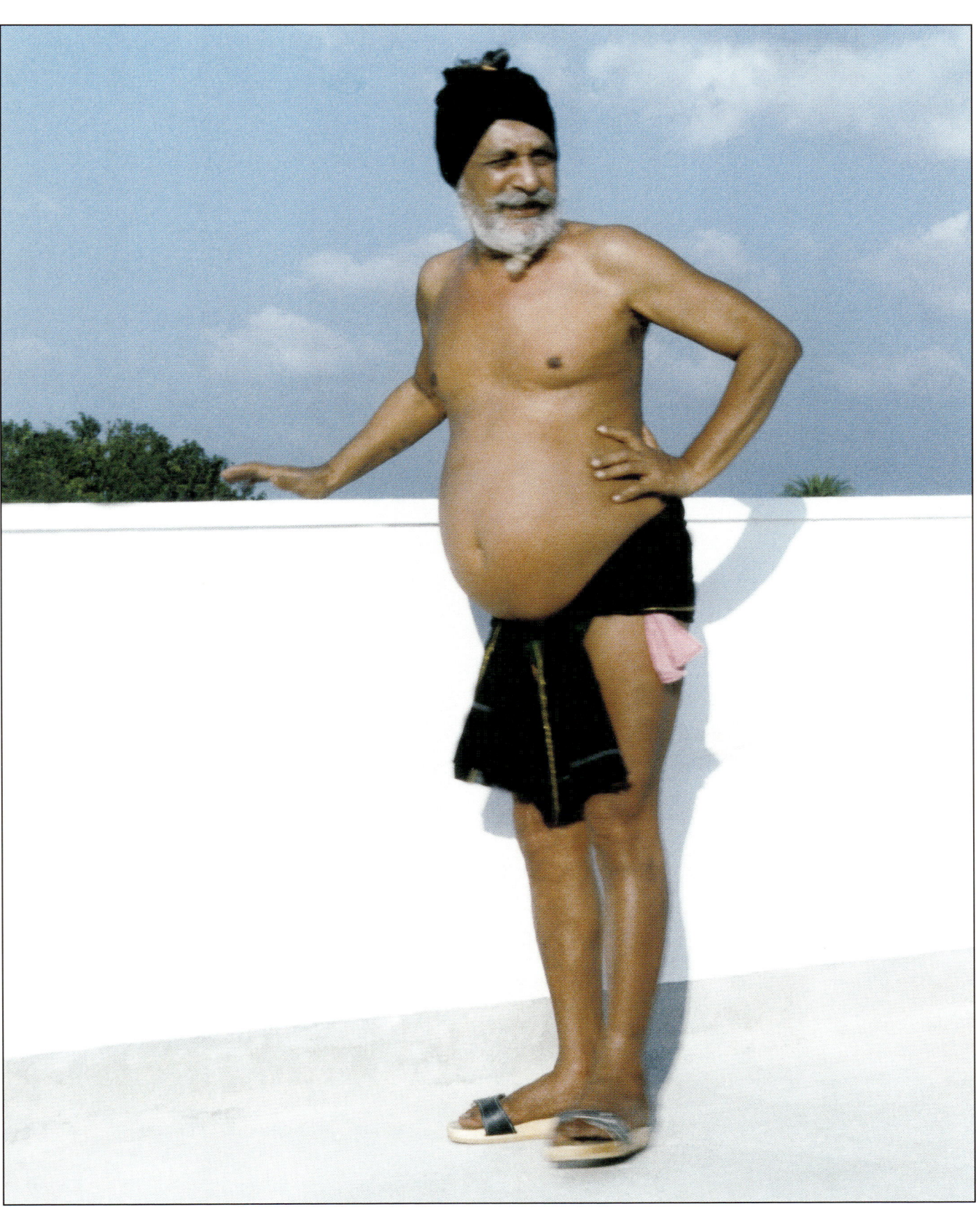

1995

Sat Chandi Mahayajna
Rajasooya Yajna
Sita Kalyanam

१९९६

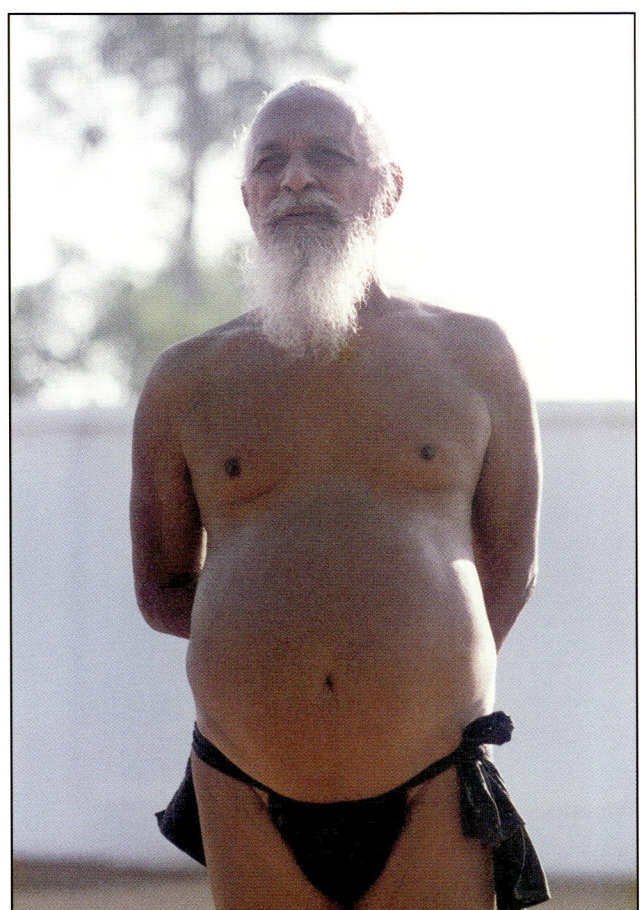

1998

2002

2004

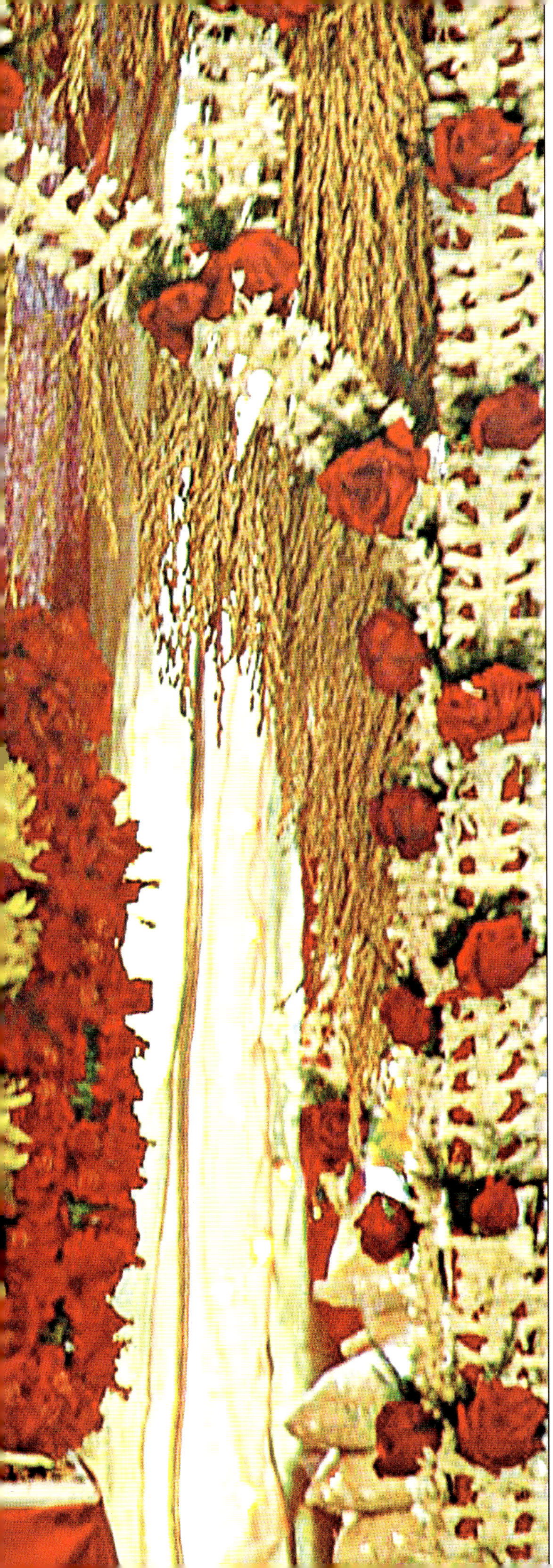

2005

2006

2007...

The Tirth Yatra continues...

Synopsis of the Life of Swami Satyananda Saraswati

Swami Satyananda Saraswati was born in 1923 at Almora (Uttaranchal) into a family of farmers. His ancestors were warriors and many of his kith and kin down the line, including his father, served in the army and police force.

However, it became evident that Sri Swamiji had a different bent of mind, as he began to have spiritual experiences at the age of six, when his awareness spontaneously left the body and he saw himself lying motionless on the floor. Many saints and sadhus blessed him and reassured his parents that he had a very developed awareness. This experience of disembodied awareness continued, which led him to many saints of that time such as Anandamayi Ma. Sri Swamiji also met a tantric bhairavi, Sukhman Giri, who gave him *shaktipat*, transmission of energy, and directed him to find a guru in order to stabilize his spiritual experiences.

In 1943, at the age of 20, he renounced his home and went in search of a guru. This search ultimately led him to Swami Sivananda Saraswati at Rishikesh, who initiated him into the Dashnami order of sannyasa on 12th September 1947 on the banks of the Ganges and gave him the name of Swami Satyananda Saraswati.

In those early years at Rishikesh, Sri Swamiji immersed himself in guru seva. At that time the ashram was still in its infancy and even the basic amenities such as buildings and toilets were absent. The forests surrounding the small ashram were infested with snakes, scorpions, mosquitoes, monkeys and even tigers. The ashram work too was heavy and hard, requiring Sri Swamiji to toil like a labourer carrying bucket loads of water from the Ganga up to the ashram and digging canals from the high mountain streams down to the ashram many kilometres away, in order to store water for constructing the ashram.

Rishikesh was then a small town and all the ashram requirements had to be brought by foot from far away. In addition there were varied duties, including the daily pooja at Vishwanath Mandir, for which Sri Swamiji would go into the dense forests to collect bael leaves. If anyone fell sick there was no medical care and no one to attend to them. All the sannyasins had to go out for bhiksha or alms as the ashram did not have a mess or kitchen.

Of that glorious time when he lived and served his guru, Sri Swamiji says that it was a period of total communion and surrender to the guru tattwa, whereby he felt that just to hear, speak of or see Swami Sivananda was yoga. But most of all through his nishkama seva he gained an enlightened understanding of the secrets of spiritual life and became an authority on yoga, tantra, Vedanta, Samkhya and kundalini yoga. Swami Sivananda said of Swami Satyananda, "Few would exhibit such intense vairagya at such an early age. Swami Satyananda is full of the Nachiketa element." Although he had a photographic memory, a keen intellect, and his guru described him as a versatile genius, Swami Satyananda's learning did not come from books and study in the ashram. His knowledge unfolded from within through his untiring seva as well as his abiding faith and love for Swami Sivananda, who told him, "Work hard and you will be purified. You do not have to search for the light; the light will unfold from within you."

In 1956, after spending twelve years in guru seva, Swami Satyananda set out as a wanderer (*parivrajaka*). Before his departure Swami Sivananda taught him kriya yoga and gave him the mission to "spread yoga from door to door and shore to shore".

As a wandering sannyasin, Swami Satyananda travelled extensively by foot, train, horse, boat, bullock-cart and elephant throughout India, Afghanistan, Burma, Nepal and Ceylon. During his sojourns, he met people from all strata of society and began formulating his ideas on how to spread the yogic techniques. Although his formal education and spiritual tradition was that of Vedanta, the task of disseminating yoga became his movement.

His mission unfolded before him in 1962 when he founded the International Yoga Fellowship Movement with the aim of creating a global fraternity of yoga. As his mission was revealed to him at Munger, Bihar, he established the Bihar School of Yoga in Munger. Before long his teachings were rapidly spreading throughout the world. From 1963 to 1982, Swami Satyananda took yoga to each and every corner of the world, to people of every caste, creed, religion and nationality. He guided millions of seekers in all continents and established centres and ashrams in different countries.

His frequent travel took him to Australia, New Zealand, Japan, China, the Philippines, Hong Kong, Malaysia, Thailand, Singapore, USA, England, Ireland, France, Italy, Germany, Switzerland, Denmark, Sweden, Yugoslavia, Poland, Hungary, Bulgaria, Slovenia, Russia, Czechoslovakia, Greece, Saudi Arabia, Kuwait, Bahrain, Dubai, Iraq, Iran, Pakistan, Afghanistan, Colombia, Brazil, Uruguay, Chile, Argentina, Santo Domingo, Puerto Rico, Sudan, Egypt, Nairobi, Ghana, Mauritius, Alaska and Iceland. One can easily say that Sri Swamiji hoisted the flag of yoga in every nook and cranny of the world.

Nowhere did he face opposition, resistance or criticism. His way was unique. Well-versed in all religions and scriptures, he incorporated their wisdom with such a natural flair that people of all faiths were drawn to him. His teaching was not just confined to yoga but covered the wisdom of many millenniums.

Sri Swamiji brought to light the knowledge of tantra, the mother of all philosophies, the sublime truths of Vedanta, the Upanishads and Puranas, Buddhism, Jainism, Sikhism, Zoroastrianism, Islam and Christianity, including a modern scientific analysis of matter and creation. He interpreted, explained and gave precise, accurate and systematic explanations of the ancient systems of tantra and yoga, revealing practices hitherto unknown.

It can be said that Sri Swamiji was a pioneer in the field of yoga because his presentation had a novelty and freshness. Ajapa japa, antar mouna, pawanmuktasana, kriya yoga and prana vidya are just some of the practices which he introduced in such a methodical and simple manner that it became possible for everyone to delve into this valuable and hitherto inaccessible science for their physical, mental, emotional and spiritual development.

Yoga nidra was Sri Swamiji's interpretation of the tantric system of nyasa. With his deep insight into this knowledge, he was able to realize the potential of this practice of nyasa in a manner which gave it a practical utility for each and every individual, rather than just remaining a prerequisite for worship. Yoga nidra is but one example of his acumen and penetrating insight into the ancient systems.

Sri Swamiji's outlook was inspiring, uplifting as well as in-depth and penetrating. Yet his language and explanations were always simple and easy to comprehend. During this period he authored over eighty books on yoga and tantra which, due to their authenticity, are accepted as textbooks in schools and universities throughout the world. These books have been translated into Italian, German, Spanish, Russian, Yugoslavian, Chinese, French, Greek, Iranian and most other prominent languages of the world.

People took to his ideas and spiritual seekers of all faiths and nationalities flocked to him. He initiated thousands into mantra and sannyasa, sowing in them the seed to live the divine life. He exhibited tremendous zeal and energy in spreading the light of yoga, and in the short span of twenty years Sri Swamiji fulfilled the mandate of his guru.

Thus, by 1983, Swami Satyananda's tireless efforts to spread the message of yoga had touched the whole world. He had also trained a core of sannyasins to transmit the yogic techniques for different needs and cultures, and they had established many Satyananda Yoga ashrams, schools and centres around India and the world. Bihar School of Yoga was well established and recognized throughout the world as a reputed and authentic centre for learning yoga and the spiritual sciences. More than that, yoga had moved out of the caves of hermits and ascetics into the mainstream of society. Whether in hospitals, jails, schools, colleges, business houses, the sporting and fashion arenas, the army or navy, yoga was in demand. Scientific research into yogic techniques was being conducted all over the world. Professionals such as lawyers, engineers, doctors, business magnates and professors were incorporating yoga into their lives. So too were the masses. Yoga had become a household word.

Then, at the peak of his accomplishment, Sri Swamiji renounced all that he created. He appointed Swami Niranjanananda as his successor and gave him the mandate to continue the work, and then began to gradually withdraw from the teaching and administering of the yoga movement. In 1988, Sri Swamiji renounced disciples, establishments and institutions, and departed from Munger, never to return again. He went on a pilgrimage through the *siddha teerthas* (spiritual centres) of India as a mendicant, without any personal belonging or assistance from the ashram or institutions he had founded.

At Tryambakeshwar, before the jyotirlingam of Lord Mrityunjaya, his ishta devata, he renounced his garb and lived as an avadhoota. And here, at the source of the Godavari River near Neel Parbat, while performing chaturmas anushthana, his future place of abode and sadhana were revealed to him. He received the mandate for a new mission, to progress toward the cosmic dimension through unbroken remembrance and repetition of the Lord's name with every breath. On 8th September, 1989, birthday of his guru Swami Sivananda, he heard the voice loud and clear, "Chitabhoomi", and saw a vision of the place where he was intended to go.

Swami Satyananda did not choose Rikhia, it was chosen for him. After leaving Munger, while roaming the length and breadth of India, he came across many beautiful places where he was invited to take up residence. However, in keeping with his style of surrender he awaited the mandate of his ishta and guru, which guided him to the small nondescript, unknown village of Rikhia, on the outskirts of Baba Baidyanath Dham in Deoghar (Jharkhand), the *chitabhoomi* or cremation ground of Sati, consort of Shiva.

Sri Swamiji arrived at Rikhia on 23rd September 1989, at midday, the day of vernal equinox, when nature is in perfect balance as the day and night are equal. Soon after, he lit a *dhuni* or fire and called it Mahakal Chita Dhuni. Lighting a dhuni is a very ancient tradition among sadhus. It is believed that the ash from a sadhu's dhuni is very potent, for his entire day is spent in front of the dhuni and all his acts are performed with the fire as witness.

The Rikhia that Swami Satyananda arrived in was still living in the sixteenth century. There were no roads, electricity, telephones, newspapers, television or shops. However, its vibrations were pure and spiritual, providing an ideal climate for the seclusion which he imposed on himself. He began a life of intensive spiritual practice, entering the lifestyle of paramahamsas who do not work for their flock and mission alone, but have a universal vision. His first anushthana commenced in 1989 during Ashwin Navaratri: the performance of ashtottar-shat-laksh (108 lakh) mantra purascharana which took him three hundred days to complete. He gave up the geru cloth and donned the kaupeen, loin cloth, an important hallmark in the life of a sadhu denoting that vairagya and dispassion are an inherent part of his being. He no longer associated with any institutions, nor gave diksha, upadesh or received dakshina, but remained in seclusion and sadhana.

In a conclusive message, he told all, "I have nothing more to say to anyone and no further guidance to give. For over twenty years I have lived with the people answering their questions and helping them on their spiritual path. Now I withdraw my responsibility. Those who are receptive, they will surely benefit from what I have told them, but those who are not, they will now have to find their own way."

In 1990, he designated the sadhana sthal as Sri Panch Dashnam Paramahamsa Alakh Bara, denoting it as a place where a sannyasin who has perfected himself consolidates his learning and gives it momentum to attain greater spiritual heights. The *ishta devi*, presiding goddess, of the akhara was established as Tulsi Ma, the benevolent force presiding over all spheres. Now Sri Swamiji undertook the vow of *panchagni*, the five-fire austerity, in which he performed higher sadhanas sitting before five blazing fires outdoors during the hottest months of the year. The vow culminated in 1998. The fire lit by Sri Swamiji is still burning at Rikhiapeeth and is worshipped daily at sunrise and sunset with aromatic herbs amidst the chanting of vedic mantras.

In 1991, Swami Satyananda received another divine mandate: "Take care of your neighbours as I have taken care of you." Seeking to strike a balance between the personal aspect of spiritual liberation and the social aspect of helping others, he gave Swami Niranjanananda a new task for Sivananda Math: service to and improvement of the living conditions of the tribal people in the thousands of villages surrounding Rikhiadham. Thus, from 1991 onwards, Sivananda Math undertook to finance and construct homes for the homeless, provide for clean drinking water, essential medical facilities, free clothing and household items. In the second phase of assistance, means of sustainable livelihood were provided.

In 1994, in a month-long darshan, Sri Swamiji gave a new message, of bhakti yoga. He said that the purpose of human life is to realize God through love and to serve God by helping humanity. He prophesied that while hatha yoga and raja yoga were the panacea of the twentieth century, devotion to God and bhakti yoga would be the panacea of the twenty-first.

In 1995, Sri Swamiji held the first Sat Chandi Maha Yajna, invoking the Cosmic Mother through a tantric ceremony hitherto not witnessed by common people. During this event, Sri Swamiji also passed on his spiritual and sannyasa sankalpa to Swami Niranjanananda.

In 1996, the annual event included Rama Naam Aradhana and Sita-Rama Vivaha, and in 1997, Sri Swamiji declared it as Sita Kalyanam. In 2001, for the first time he revealed that the yajna was part of the 12-year Rajasooya Yajna, a ceremony that is traditionally performed by a conqueror.

"I am performing the Rajasooya Yajna not as a conqueror of land, wealth or people, but because I was able to establish an empire of yoga, which is the need of today in our civilization," said Sri Swamiji. "Yoga works at the spiritual, mental and physical levels to improve the quality of life, and that is also the concept of prosperity in today's society. We have wealth, but we lack quality of life and peace of mind. I am performing the Rajasooya Yajna to re-establish peace of mind, to re-equip people with the riches of contentment, happiness, joy and wellbeing."

In 1998, Sri Swamiji also inspired Sivananda Math to undertake an education project. Thus scholarships were given to deserving students of Rikhia panchayat with special emphasis on the education of girls. English classes were also started at the ashram. By 2001, nearly all eligible children aged between 6–12 years of Rikhia panchayat had been adopted into the ever-expanding family of Swami Satyananda. In 2003, computer training was started. The girls, called *kanyas*, were also taught chanting of Sanskrit stotras. The boys, *batuks*, were simultaneously introduced to Gayatri mantra, Bhagavad Gita, surya namaskara, and rituals of havan and worship. Today these little children confidently conduct all the ceremonies and rituals at Rikhiapeeth before thousands of devotees who come to participate in these events.

In 2004, Sivananda Ashram was formed with the main thrust of looking after the elderly and infirm, including widows. It has also undertaken a project to provide one wholesome meal a day to the children and elderly of Rikhia panchayat.

Thus, in a short span of time, a silent revolution has taken place in Rikhia. It was all made possible by a sannyasin who came to this place to live in solitude. Sri Swamiji says, "After coming to Rikhia my cataracted vision was corrected. I have lived a spiritual life for more than sixty years. I have practised every form of yoga, but ultimately I found that when I began to think about others, God began to think about me. On my guru's instructions, I lit the flame of yoga in Munger and the light of seva in Rikhia. This is the requirement of humanity today."

In 2007, Sri Swamiji announced the formation of Rikhiapeeth. He said, "The Rikhia ashram will now be known as Rikhiapeeth. Peeth means 'seat', an apt term for Rikhia as the instructions given to me by Swami Sivananda have culminated and fructified here. Rikhia is an ashram in the original sense of the word because here a lifestyle is lived. Swami Satyasangananda is the Peethadhishwari of Rikhiapeeth and has been given the sankalpa that the three cardinal teachings of Swami Sivananda, serve, love and give, will be practised and lived here. This is the future vision of Rikhiapeeth."

In 2009, after participating in and giving darshan during Sat Chandi Mahayajna and Yoga Poornima where Sri Swamiji inspired everyone to lead the righteous life and bid final farewell to the thousands who had gathered to participate in these events, he entered into mahasamadhi on the midnight of 5th December and merged into Swami Sivananda, our sadguru.

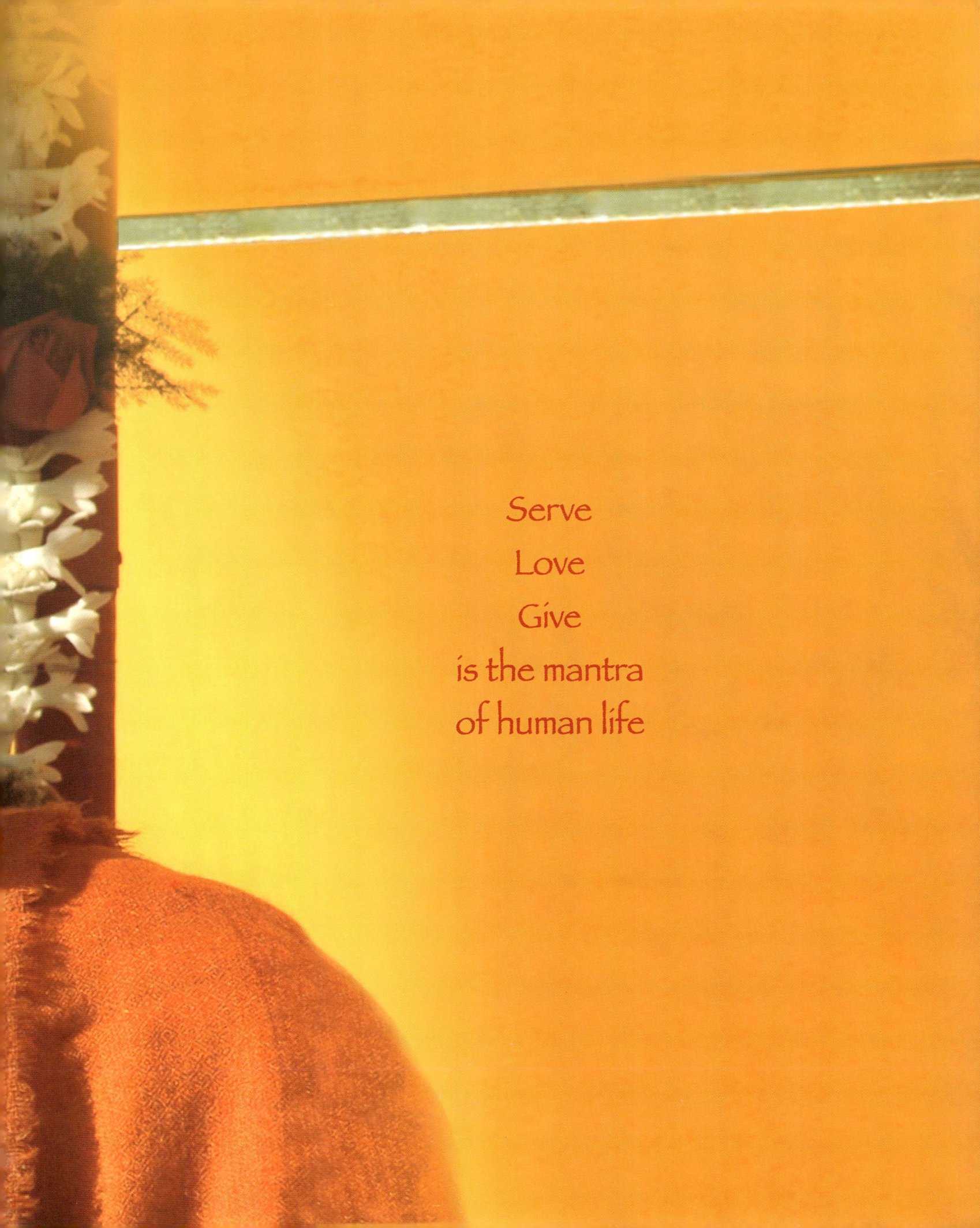

Serve
Love
Give
is the mantra
of human life

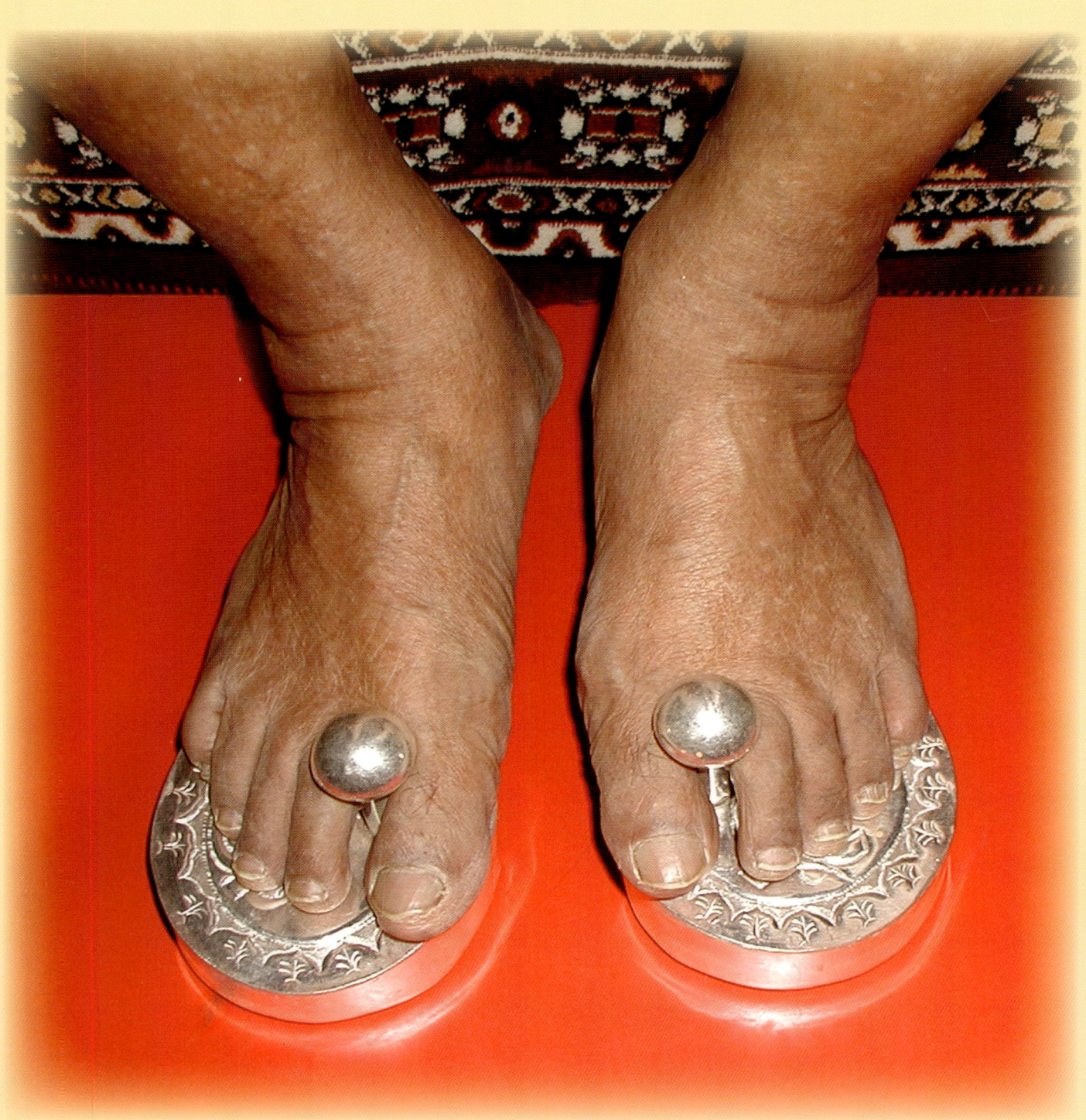

अनन्तसंसारसमुद्रतार-
नौकायिताभ्यां गुरूभक्तिदाभ्याम् ।
वैराग्यसाम्राज्यदपूजनाभ्यां
नमो नमः श्रीगुरुपादुकाभ्याम् ॥

कवित्ववाराशिनिशाकराभ्यां
दौर्भाग्यदवाम्बुदमालिकाभ्याम् ।
दूरीकृतानम्रविपत्तिताभ्यां
नमो नमः श्रीगुरुपादुकाभ्याम् ॥

नता ययोः श्रीपतितां समीयुः
कदाचिदप्याशु दरिद्रवर्याः ।
मूकाश्च वाचस्पतितां हि ताभ्यां
नमो नमः श्रीगुरुपादुकाभ्याम् ॥

नालीकनीकाशपदाहृताभ्यां
नानाविमोहादि निवारिकाभ्याम् ।
नमज्जनाभीष्टततिप्रदाभ्यां
नमो नमः श्रीगुरुपादुकाभ्याम् ॥

नृपालिमौलिव्रजरत्नकान्ति-
सरिद्विराजज्झषकन्यकाभ्याम् ।
नृपत्वदाभ्यां नतलोकपंक्तेः
नमो नमः श्रीगुरुपादुकाभ्याम् ॥

पापान्धकारार्क परम्पराभ्यां
तापत्रयाहीन्द्रखगेश्वराभ्याम् ।
जाड्याब्धिसंशोषणवाडवाभ्यां
नमो नमः श्रीगुरुपादुकाभ्याम् ॥

शमादिषट्कप्रदवैभवाभ्यां
समाधिदानव्रतदीक्षिताभ्याम् ।
रमाधवांघ्रिस्थिरभक्तिदाभ्यां
नमो नमः श्रीगुरुपादुकाभ्याम् ॥

स्वार्चापराणामखिलेष्टदाभ्यां
स्वाहासहायाक्षधुरन्धराभ्याम् ।
स्वान्ताच्छभावप्रद पूजनाभ्यां
नमो नमः श्रीगुरुपादुकाभ्याम् ॥

कामादिसर्पव्रजगारुडाभ्यां
विवेकवैराग्यनिधिप्रदाभ्याम् ।
बोधप्रदाभ्यां द्रुतमोक्षदाभ्यां
नमो नमः श्रीगुरुपादुकाभ्याम् ॥

Anantasamsārasamudratāra-
Naukāyitābhyāṃ gurubhaktidābhyām.
Vairāgyasāmrājyadapūjanābhyām
Namo namaḥ śrīgurupādukābhyām.

Kavitvavārāśiniśākarābhyām
Daurbhāgyadāvāmbudamālikābhyām.
Dūrīkṛtānamravipattitābhyām
Namo namaḥ śrīgurupādukābhyām.

Natā yayoḥ śrīpatitāṃ samīyuḥ
kadāchidapyāśu daridravaryāḥ.
Mūkāścha vāchaspatitāṃ hi tabhyām
Namo namaḥ śrīgurupādukābhyām.

Nālīkanīkāśapadāhṛtābhyām
Nānāvimohādi nivārikābhyām.
Namajjanābhīṣṭatatipradābhyām
Namo namaḥ śrīgurupādukābhyām.

Nṛpālimaulivrajaratnakānti-
Saridvirājajjhaṣakanyakābhyām.
Nṛpatvadābhyām natalokapaṅkteḥ
Namo namaḥ śrīgurupādukābhyām.

Pāpāndhakārārka paramparābhyām
Tāpatrayāhīndrakhageśvarābhyām.
Jāḍyābdhisaṃśoṣaṇavāḍavābhyām
Namo namaḥ śrīgurupādukābhyām.

Śamādiṣaṭkapradavaibhavābhyām
Samādhidānavratadīkṣitābhyām.
Ramādhavāṅghristhirabhaktidābhyām
Namo namaḥ śrīgurupādukābhyām.

Svārchāparāṇāmakhileṣṭadābhyām
Svāhāsahāyakṣadhurandharābhyām.
Svāntāchchhabhāvaprada pūjanābhyām
Namo namaḥ śrīgurupādukābhyām.

Kāmādisarpavrajagāruḍābhyām
Vivekavairāgyanidhipradābhyām.
Bodhapradābhyāṃ drutamokṣadābhyām
Namo namaḥ śrīgurupādukābhyām.

Institutions Inspired by Swami Satyananda Saraswati

International Yoga Fellowship Movement (IYFM), 1956

Bihar School of Yoga (BSY), 1963

Sivananda Math (SM), 1984

Yoga Research Foundation (YRF), 1984

Sri Panchdashnam Paramahamsa Alakh Bara (PPAB), 1989

Bihar Yoga Bharati (BYB), 1994

Yoga Publications Trust (YPT), 2000

Sivananda Ashram (SA), 2006

Rikhiapeeth, 2007

Sannyasa Peeth, 2010

We are your creations,
We are your visions,
We are your aspirations,
Grant us wisdom to know the appropriate,
Grant us determination to do the appropriate,
Let your grace flow through us . . .